A STUDY GUIDE

FOR

JOSEPH RATZINGER'S
(POPE BENEDICT XVI)

JESUS
OF NAZARETH

FROM THE BAPTISM IN THE JORDAN
TO THE TRANSFIGURATION

Introduction by
Mark Brumley, M.T.S.

Outlines by
Matthew Levering, Ph.D.

Summaries, Terms, and Questions by
Thomas Harmon, M.A. and Laura Dittus, M.A.

IGNATIUS PRESS   SAN FRANCISCO

Cover art: *Salvator Mundi,* Joos van Cleve (1485–1540)
Louvre, Paris, France
© Réunion des Musées Nationaux / Art Resource, New York

Cover design by Roxanne Mei Lum

Contents

Introduction to This Study Guide

This booklet aims to help the average reader who approaches *Jesus of Nazareth* without the benefit of extensive theological or biblical training to get as much out of the work as possible. The goal is not to replace the book, but to make it more accessible and more fruitful.

To that end, this introduction is divided into two parts. The first part surveys some key ideas important to understanding *Jesus of Nazareth*; the second explains how to use the various features of this booklet for individual or group study.

The fact that *Jesus of Nazareth* is an important book does not make it an "easy read" for everyone. Although not a scholarly treatise, it is also not a popular "life of Christ". Instead, it is a book that addresses the average, informed reader in light of modern scholarly discussions about Jesus and the Bible. To understand *Jesus of Nazareth*, it helps if readers know a bit about some of the important controversies in biblical studies in the last hundred years.

Christianity Is a Historical Religion

Readers who do not follow the "ins" and "outs" of theology or biblical scholarship are sometimes perplexed or even disturbed by what is called the historical-critical method. Benedict calls it "an indispensible tool" (xv, xvi), yet he also cautions about its use. To understand why, we need a little background.

Christianity, as Benedict emphasizes, is a historical religion (xv). It is not about myths or cosmic principles expressed symbolically in fictional form, but about real people, real places, and real events. To the extent that Christianity can be called a myth, it is, as C. S. Lewis and J. R. R. Tolkien put it, a "true myth". That is, it is a story with all the grandeur of myth but with all the factualness of history: it really happened. The Incarnation of the Son of God, the central truth of Christianity, is "myth become fact", to use Lewis' expression. And the central fact of Christianity is the fact of God acting in human history in the Person of Jesus of Nazareth.

Because Christianity is about certain events of history—the life, death, and Resurrection of Jesus Christ and the establishment of his Church—historical scholarship has a role to play in our understanding of the accounts of those events, which are found in the four Gospels (Matthew, Mark, Luke, and John). Traditional Christianity holds these writings to be the divinely-inspired records of the life and teaching of Jesus. Like other records, they have their own histories of composition and contexts in which they were written. Historical scholarship can help us understand Jesus by helping us appreciate the historical context of the Gospels—for example, what the original Gospel writers meant, what their sources may have been, who their intended audiences were, and what distinctive elements each Gospel writer brought to his presentation of Jesus and his teaching.

Even so, as Benedict points out, the conclusions of historical scholarship are not always certain (xvii, xix). Indeed, such conclusions often change as more information is obtained or as old arguments are reviewed and judged deficient. One age's certainties about the past become another age's discarded theories. It is not history itself that changes—whatever happened happened. It is our *understanding* of history—what we can show from evidence, for instance, or how we view certain historical documents—that changes.

Historical-Critical Method and Biblical Criticism

Terms such as "historical-critical method" and "biblical criticism" sometimes concern, even alarm, believers because of what these expressions seem to imply. To many people, it sounds as if the Bible is being "criticized", as if man is sitting in judgment on the Word of God. Some believers worry that the Word of God is being forsaken for the sake of "human traditions" and "vain philosophies".

The fact is, some scholars *do* approach the Bible as if it were a collection of merely human writings, and these scholars are not bashful about subjecting Scripture to "critical" scrutiny the way other merely human documents are evaluated. Furthermore, these scholars often have ideological axes to grind against traditional Christian beliefs, and they go out of their way to undermine the credibility of those portions of Scripture that support those beliefs.

For other scholars, though, the "critical" part of the "historical-critical method" does not imply that the Bible should be understood as a collection of merely human documents. "Critical", as these scholars understand the term, refers to a systematic analysis of the biblical texts, in light of historical knowledge, in order to come to historically-grounded conclusions about such issues as what the biblical authors intended, what their sources may have been, how they have highlighted or applied Jesus' teaching to their communities, and how the biblical books were put together. For them, "critical" means a careful, methodical, systematic process of trying to understand the texts in terms of what their authors intended.

It is this second sense of the "historical-critical method" that Benedict says is "indispensible", although even in this sense Benedict still sees the method as limited and in need of other principles in order for it to enable us to encounter the full reality of

Scripture as divinely inspired and as God's Word speaking to us today, not merely a record of the past (xvi–xxiii).

As valuable as historical scholarship can be, our appreciation of the Gospels as inspired sources for the life and teaching of Jesus does not ultimately rest on scholarly findings or arguments, which are subject to debate, revision, and abandonment over time. Historical interpretations and arguments may change, but the fundamental realities of Jesus Christ and his teaching do not change. Historical scholarship may help deepen our understanding of Jesus Christ, but its findings cannot alter the essential truth about him anymore than discovering a new species of insect or finding a new particle of matter can change the fact that God created the world.

The Gospels are, in the final analysis, more than merely human records; they are part of God's Word to us. Benedict stresses that Scripture is both a divinely inspired expression *of* the Church's faith—it shows us what the Church believes—and the Word of God expressed in written form *to* the Church and *for* the Church. The Church remains the "subject" of the Bible (xxi)—that is, the one to whom the Bible is addressed and through whom it is properly understood. Through reflecting upon Scripture, the Church grows in her understanding and possession of what God has revealed. In this way, she deepens her union with Christ and, through him, her union with the Father in the Holy Spirit.

The divine aspect of the Bible means that the Church can and must go beyond the findings of historical scholarship. That does not mean that something can be true as a matter of history, but not true when it comes to the Church's faith, or true as a matter of the Church's faith, but not true as a matter of history. Just the opposite. The unity of truth means that what is true as a matter of historical research cannot ultimately conflict with what is true as a matter of revelation and faith.

The "Jesus of History" and the "Christ of Faith"

This brings us to the distinction often made today between the "Jesus of history" and the "Christ of faith". Pope Benedict addresses the distinction early in *Jesus of Nazareth*—in the second paragraph of the foreword (xi). The distinction can be understood in different ways, so we should take some time to be clear about it.

When people speak of the "Jesus of history", they can mean "Jesus as he really was". "History" then means "what really happened in the past or the way things or people really were". However, the "Jesus of history" can also mean "Jesus as historical research has been able to show him to have been". That is not the same thing as "Jesus as he really was".

Who someone was is one thing; who we *can show* from historical research that a person was is something else. Why? Because not everything true of a person of the past can *be shown* by historical evidence to have been true. Documents can be faked or misinterpreted, memories can fade or become confused, evidence can be lost. Consequently, sometimes we can come up with only a small piece of the genuine past.

And, even when documents can be shown to be authentic or properly understood, when memories are sound, and when ample evidence remains, there can be other problems. For instance, sometimes people trying very hard to be unbiased can let prejudice affect their judgments. As a result, their judgments about some past figure or event may be wrong or incomplete.

In biblical scholarship a major difficulty can be the prior theological or philosophical commitment of a particular scholar. If, for instance, as a matter of his personal philosophy, a scholar holds that miracles are impossible, then he will not interpret as historically accurate those documents that purport to record miracles. He will find another explanation. If miracles are possible, and if in fact the accounts that purport to record certain miracles are accurate, he will not know it because his prior commitment to a "miracles are impossible" worldview will force him to explain away reports of the miraculous.

Similarly, a scholar may have certain ideas about how the early Christian view of Jesus must have developed. Such a scholar may think that Christians only began to think of Jesus as divine after five or six decades. That view will influence how he assesses the historical reliability of certain statements in the Gospels.

But even when we have reliable evidence, reasonably impartial testimony, and no philosophical commitments that preclude accepting the evidence, historical research can give us only a bit of the truth about a person or an event of the past. A great deal of who a person is or what he is like cannot be gleaned from evidence or testimony. Even under the best circumstances, then, much of the past is out of the historian's reach.

We must, therefore, distinguish "Jesus as he really was" from "Jesus as historians can show him to have been". "Jesus as he really was" is a much larger reality than "Jesus as historians can show him to have been" because no amount of historical research can "capture" the whole of a person from the past.

Of course, historians like to think that their reconstructions are accurate. While they will admit that historical research cannot tell us everything about someone from history, they are often very confident that their reconstructions are as accurate as historical reconstructions can be. This is the situation with many historical-critical scholars and the "Jesus of history". Each is certain that his historical reconstruction is correct. And yet, as Benedict points out (xii), often these historical reconstructions conflict with one another because they reflect the scholars who create them more than Jesus.

What about the expression the "Christ of faith"? Usually, this is understood to refer to what believers say about Jesus. The "Christ of faith" is what "the Church"— understood as those who identify with the mainstream of traditional Christian belief— believes about Jesus' life, his teaching, his death, and his Resurrection.

You may wonder how traditional Christian belief about Jesus is different from "Jesus as he really was". If so, you are probably a traditional Christian. Traditional Christianity— Catholic, Orthodox, and Protestant—holds that the "Christ of faith" *is* the "Jesus of history", at least in the sense of "Jesus as he really was". If there is a distinction to be made between the "Jesus of history" and the "Christ of faith", according to traditional

Christianity, it is not between Jesus as he was and Jesus as the Church believes him to be. It is the distinction between what historical scholarship can tell us, which is not everything, and what the faith of the Church affirms, which goes well beyond what historians can prove, even though it must ultimately be compatible with it.

Opinions vary among traditional Christian scholars on exactly how much of what traditional Christians affirm about Jesus can be demonstrated from historical argumentation alone and the extent to which the way the Gospel writers or their sources have, based on more theologically mature perspectives and the concerns of their respective communities, shaped their accounts of Jesus. Nevertheless, traditional Christians agree that the "Christ of faith" is Jesus of Nazareth, who really lived, taught, died, and rose from the dead two thousand years ago, and that the Gospel depictions of him, properly understood and interpreted in their historical contexts, are historically trustworthy.

Not everyone who identifies himself with Christianity or who is interested in Jesus would agree that the "Christ of faith" is the same person as "Jesus as he really was". Some scholars hold that many traditional Christian ideas about Jesus have nothing to do with "the real Jesus"—the "historical Jesus" or the "Jesus of history". Traditional Christian beliefs, so such scholars contend, developed gradually as new ideas and interpretations of Jesus emerged and people lost contact with the historical person. Historical scholarship, on this view, tries to peel away various layers of interpretation to get at what is supposed to be the true Jesus—a Jesus who did not do or say the kind of things attributed to him by the Gospel writers.

We see, then, that there are two basic positions regarding the distinction between the "Jesus of history" and the "Christ of faith". The first position acknowledges that there is a difference between what historical scholarship can document or prove and what the Church believes, even though the "Jesus of history" and the "Christ of faith" are thought to be the same person. The two ideas complement rather than contradict each other, notwithstanding the fact that the Church's faith paints a fuller picture of "the real Jesus" than the results of historical scholarship alone reveal.

The second view of the relationship between the "Jesus of history" and the "Christ of faith" holds that Jesus, as historians reconstruct him to have been, is closer to the "real Jesus" than the "Christ of faith", who comes from the Church's preaching. The latter view involves various modifications, misunderstandings, and distortions of the "historical Jesus". Critical scholarship alone, so the argument goes, enables us to know Jesus as he really was by peeling off the various layers of tradition that the Gospels contain.

Although the two views above both distinguish the "Jesus of history" from the "Christ of faith", they do so in crucially different ways. It is one thing to say that historical research alone cannot show the truth of everything the Church says about Jesus. It is another thing to say that historical research leads us to think that Jesus was different from what the Church believes about him. Not everything the Church believes can be proved or shown to be highly probable by historical research, but it is a problem if historical research can disprove what the Church believes about Jesus or show it to be highly improbable.

Benedict, as he indicates in his foreword, "trusts the Gospels" (xxi) as reliable, even though he acknowledges the value of modern scholarship, the importance of distinguishing literary genres, etc. This is not a fundamentalistic dismissal of historical criticism or a "blind faith" refusal to face alternative claims. Benedict holds that the Jesus of the Gospels *is* the Jesus of history because Benedict believes the former to be more historically plausible and more rational than the various reconstructions of Jesus that purport to be "scientific" and based on history (xxii).

Not a Work of the Magisterium

The author of *Jesus of Nazareth* offers a number of theological judgments and opinions about the life and teaching of Jesus, as well as how the Gospels should be interpreted. It just so happens that the author is the Bishop of Rome, the Pope. How should readers understand the various judgments and opinions Benedict XVI offers in his book? Do they reflect "the teaching of the Catholic Church"?

Not as such. In other words, simply because Benedict takes a position on a theological issue in *Jesus of Nazareth* does not mean that this position is "the teaching of the Catholic Church". Of course some of the things Benedict discusses are Catholic teaching. However, they are such for reasons other than that they happen to appear in *Jesus of Nazareth*. They are taught elsewhere as official Catholic doctrine.

Benedict XVI indicates that he does not want his theological opinions in *Jesus of Nazareth* to be understood as an exercise of the Magisterium, the teaching office of the Catholic Church (xxiii). To be sure, he thinks the positions he presents in the book are true and compatible with Catholic teaching, but he wants readers to accept his positions on the basis of the arguments he makes for them, rather than on the basis of his authority as the Bishop of Rome. In other words, *Jesus of Nazareth* is the work of a theologian who happens to be the Pope, not a document of the Pope of the Catholic Church. While Catholics are free, as Benedict says, to disagree with his arguments (xxiv), they (and all other readers) should be willing to give due deference to the judgments of an expert on the subject, which Benedict is, as they would give deference to the judgment of experts in other fields.

How to Use This Study Guide

For each of the twelve sections of *Jesus of Nazareth*—foreword, introduction, and ten chapters—there is a corresponding section with (1) a summary of the section or chapter; (2) an outline; (3) a list of important terms; (4) study/discussion questions; and (5) an area for readers to include their personal reflections on the reading. Also included in this study guide is a glossary of key terms.

The resources of this booklet can be used for individual study and reflection or for group study and discussion. Group study can easily be divided into twelve sessions, corresponding to the twelve sections of *Jesus of Nazareth*. The following structure is recommended for each group session.

- Opening prayer
- Reading summary aloud
- Discussion of summary
- Review of questions for discussion or discussion of particular passages of the text
- Comments on personal reflection
- Closing prayer

Large numbers often pose problems for group discussion. Those interested in using this booklet with study groups may want to limit the group size to between three and twenty people. In parish settings, it might be helpful to create more than one study group.

We hope that through this study guide and through the work of Benedict XVI that you may be led to encounter Christ more deeply and evermore to "seek his face" (cf. Ps 27:8).

—*Mark Brumley, M.T.S.*

The Foreword to Jesus of Nazareth

Summary

In recent years, many practitioners of what is known as the historical-critical method of biblical study have claimed that the historical Jesus was very different from the Jesus known to the Church through faith. Benedict XVI writes *Jesus of Nazareth* in order to present the Jesus of the Gospels as a plausible historical figure. In other words, he states that the Christ of faith—Jesus as the Church proclaims him to be—is the same person as the Jesus of history.

Benedict acknowledges the treasures that the historical-critical method provides both to the scholar and the layman. However, he also underscores the method's limitation it is a purely *historical* method. When it comes to providing the full truth about Jesus, the method lacks what the faith of the Church provides. As an empirical method, it is based on studying what is observable or can be discovered from the historical record alone. This excludes both spiritual and interior realities, which can neither be seen nor touched. Because it is a *historical* method, it tends to leave Jesus in the past, cutting him off from the modern believer.

The most important truth about Jesus is his communion with the Father, a reality presented to the Church in history through his words, his deeds, the Gospel, and apostolic testimonies to him—only fully understandable through faith. Communion with Jesus in the Church does not leave the real Jesus in the past, but connects the modern believer dynamically to him. Benedict will attempt throughout the book never to lose sight of faith, while at the same time availing himself of the best that historical-critical scholarship offers.

Outline

I. Are the Gospel accounts true witnesses to Jesus of Nazareth?

A. Scholarship on the historical Jesus often ends in a new portrait of Jesus, reconstructed from evidence and speculation, and differing from the Gospel portraits

B. Rudolph Schnackenburg, a prominent and believing Catholic exegete, shows both the difficulty and (in nascent form) the solution

   1. Schnackenburg views the Gospels as layers of tradition through which one has to pierce in order to catch a glimpse of Jesus of Nazareth

   2. Schnackenburg views the Gospels as witnessing to a Jesus of Nazareth who enjoyed a profound communion with God—Pope Benedict will draw out this insight in *Jesus of Nazareth*

II. Benedict's methodology in answering the above question

A. The historical-critical method provides an important contribution because Jesus lived, died, and was resurrected in human history (and thus faith cannot dispense with historical facticity)

B. The historical-critical method is limited

   1. The biblical word is never solely past, as the historical-critical method requires—the biblical truths do not have to be made present today by the exegete; rather, the biblical truths *are* present today

   2. The biblical word is not merely a human word, but a divine word that contains the possibility of being understood ever more deeply

   3. The unity of the biblical books cannot be understood through the historical method because this unity comes from God rather than being itself something that one can derive from study of each biblical book—God's ordering is what unites the various historical contexts

   4. The historical method cannot arrive at anything besides hypotheses about what happened, whereas the biblical books demand the response of faith

C. Benedict therefore gives particular approval to canonical exegesis (Brevard Childs), which reads the biblical writings both in themselves (that is, in their own historical context) and in their canonical placement and significance—canonical exegesis accords with *Dei Verbum* §12 (*Dogmatic Constitution on Divine Revelation*, from the Second Vatican Council)

   1. The key step consists in learning how to discern the unity of Scripture and its unfolding, particularly as regards the Old and New Testaments—this unity is found through faith in Christ Jesus (who is known in history)

   2. The inspiration of Scripture involves the human author speaking in a communal context that is guided by the divine Author

   3. Scripture emerges from God's relationship not to individuals, but to the People of God; the entire People of God authors and interprets Scripture, taught and guided by the divine Author

4. Scripture governs the People of God, and Scripture also lives within the People of God: this interaction between Scripture and the Church, for which the words of Scripture always bespeak present realities, belongs to the People of God's being united to God and thus transcending the limits of earthly humanity in the incarnate Christ

III. Faith and reason

A. The only way to explain the reaction of the Jewish authorities that led to Jesus' Crucifixion is that he claimed to be God, and the only way to explain Jesus' impact is his Resurrection; Benedict's approach thus goes beyond what historical-critical exegesis thinks it can show, while remaining deeply indebted to modern exegesis—faith united with historical reasoning

B. The book is not magisterial teaching, but solely Benedict's personal research

Questions for Understanding

1. What would be the significance of a cleft between the "historical Jesus" and the "Christ of faith" in light of Benedict's statement that Jesus Christ brings God to men?

2. What are the limits of the historical-critical method that Benedict seeks to overcome in *Jesus of Nazareth*? What does he say is the source of these limitations (pp. xii–xiii)?

3. Despite the historical-critical method's limitations, why does Benedict regard it as indispensable (p. xv)?

4. What does Benedict say is the key to understanding the figure of Jesus (p. xiv)?

5. How are the People of God crucial for writing, compiling, and reading the books of the Bible? What role does the inspiration of the Holy Spirit play? According to Pope Benedict, how do the People of God shed light on the doctrine of inspiration (pp. xx–xxii)?

6. What role does faith have in studying Jesus of Nazareth as the Gospels present him? What does faith bring to the study of the Bible that the historical-critical method cannot (pp. xx–xxiii)?

Questions for Application

1. What is at stake in my own life as a Christian in the debate over the "historicity" of the Gospel accounts of Jesus?

2. How does my own faith help me to read the Bible and understand Jesus?

3. How does my membership in the Church assist my understanding of the Gospel accounts of Jesus (pp. xx–xxiii)?

Terms

Karl Adam, xi
Romano Guardini, xi
Franz Michel Willam, xi
Giovanni Papini, xi
Henri Daniel-Rops, xi
"historical Jesus" and
   "Christ of faith", xi
historical-critical scholarship, xii
Rudolf Schnackenburg, xii

exegesis, xiii
Divino Afflante Spiritu, xiv
Pontifical Biblical Commission, xv
Et incarnatus est, xv
canonical exegesis, xviii
analogy of faith, xviii
inspiration, xx
infancy narratives, xxiv

─────── *Notes* ───────

The Introduction to Jesus of Nazareth

Summary

What does the future bring; what is my destiny? These fundamental questions that arise in man are not left unanswered. The answer is brought in a particular way in the Old Testament through the prophets and ultimately in Christ. Man is not to grasp for knowledge of the future through forbidden means, such as soothsaying and occult practices, but rather through turning to God who fully reveals both man and his destiny.

In the Introduction, Pope Benedict presents the figure of Christ through the lens of Deuteronomy. Here the promise of a Messiah is given not in terms of a "new David" (a king), but rather as a "new Moses" (a prophet). In Deuteronomy, the following promise is found on the lips of Moses: "The LORD your God will raise up for you a prophet like me from among you . . . him shall you heed" (Deut 18:15 as cited in *Jesus of Nazareth*). This prophecy does not point simply to a prophetic office, but rather to a "new Moses". This promise does not find its fulfillment in the time of Moses, but rather points ahead.

Pope Benedict further posits that Moses' distinguishing characteristic is his intimate friendship with God, a friendship in which he conversed with God "face to face". It is from this communion with God that Moses is enabled to perform great acts and to impart the Law. The role of the true prophet is to reveal the face of God and, in so doing, to show man the way he is to go. The true prophet is not one who merely conveys the future, but one who reveals God. In this way, the prophet is set apart from the soothsayer.

Having considered Moses and the office of the prophet, one can see how Jesus is a new Moses. Jesus is not only "like Moses", he surpasses Moses in that while Moses is only given a vision of God's "back", Jesus sees God "face to face". Jesus is the prophet *par excellence*. He reveals the face of God in a unique and unsurpassable way. By coming to know Jesus, we come to know the Father.

Outline

I. The Book of Deuteronomy

A. Jesus fulfills Deuteronomy 18:15 and 34:10, which foretell the coming of a prophet like Moses—a prophet who knows God face-to-face, but a greater prophet than Moses, because Moses only saw God's back

B. The task of the prophet is to reveal the face of God

C. Jesus as the new Moses and the mediator of a new covenant

II. The figure of Jesus

A. What Jesus teaches, he learns from the Father

B. The disciple who learns from Jesus enters into the communion of the divine Son and the Father, in the Holy Spirit

Questions for Understanding

1. What is the difference between the promise of a new David and the promise of a new Moses (p. 1)?

2. What is the difference between the prophets of Israel and the soothsayers of the surrounding peoples (pp. 2–3)?

3. Why is the ending of the Book of Deuteronomy melancholic (pp. 3–5)?

4. What is the most important characteristic of the new Moses, according to Benedict (pp. 3–4)? Why is Jesus able to carry out this role when even Moses was not able to fulfill it (p. 6)?

5. Why does Benedict say that Jesus' solitary time in prayer is crucial to understanding him?

Questions for Application

1. Do I ever succumb to the same impatience with God to which Saul fell victim? Can faith in Jesus Christ help to counteract this temptation? How (pp. 6–7)?

2. The Christian life has often been called a spiritual exodus. How does the prophetic voice of the Scriptures help to guide that exodus?

3. How were Jesus' listeners able to discern that his teaching did not come from human learning? What is it about Jesus' words that continue to provoke the same reaction even today?

4. How can I unite my own prayers to those of Christ's? Give several examples.

Terms

eschatological, 4   Adolf von Harnack, 7

Notes

CHAPTER ONE

The Baptism of Jesus

Summary

Jesus' ministry is set in a particular time and place. He comes as Israel's expected Messiah, the one who inherits God's promises to Abraham and David. He appears against the backdrop of the Roman emperors' claims to be the saviors of the human race and the bringers of earthly peace.

Jesus' baptism begins his public ministry. Jesus is the Jewish Messiah and Son of God and, consequently, the one who "takes away the sin of the world" (Jn 1:29). Jesus, the Lamb of God, will accomplish a new Passover. But this new Passover will be for the whole world and not only for Israel, as the old Passover was.

The baptism that John the Baptist administers differs from other religious washings practiced by Jews at the time. It signifies a turning once and for all from sin to fidelity and righteousness.

John baptizes Jesus "to fulfil all righteousness" (Mt 3:15). Jesus, being sinless, has no need for baptism himself. However, his baptism follows the pattern his ministry will take. In other words, in order for Jesus to take upon himself the sins of all men, he "takes their place" in his submersion into and ascent out of the waters. Jesus' baptism is therefore a sign that he takes the place of sinners, substituting himself for them. At the beginning of his ministry, Jesus already points to the Cross, where his definitive act of substituting himself for sinners takes place.

When Jesus emerges from the water, the heavens "open". This shows in a figurative way how Jesus' communion with the Father is perfect. There is a theophany, or a manifestation of God, in which the Father identifies Jesus as the Son and the Holy Spirit descends in the form of a dove. In this way, the Trinity—the Father, the Son, and the Holy Spirit—is manifested.

It is ultimately in light of Jesus' Passion, death, and Resurrection that we understand his baptism. At the same time, Jesus' baptism points ahead to the completion of Jesus' mission.

Outline

I. Salvation history and the Roman Empire

A. Genealogies of Jesus: Jesus is the inheritor of God's pledges to Abraham and David

B. Jesus is born under the Roman Empire

   1. Roman Emperors' claims to be "divine" and bringers of peace

   2. The Davidic kingdom is in ruins; God seems silent

   3. Conflicting groups in first-century Judaism: Zealots, Pharisees, Sadducees, Essenes, all of whom contribute something to Jesus' followers

II. John the Baptist

A. The baptism administered by John

   1. Fosters conversion in preparation for the Messiah's coming, including repentance and the confession of sins

   2. John's baptism with water is to be followed by baptism with "the Holy Spirit and fire"

   3. The presence of God's prophet suggests that something decisive is going to happen both for Judaism and for the Roman Empire

B. Symbolism of baptism

   1. Water symbolizes both death and life

   2. Water symbolizes purification and rebirth

III. Jesus' baptism by John the Baptist

A. Why was Jesus baptized?

   1. Jesus had no sin, but he sought to "fulfil all righteousness" by demonstrating his obedience to God—he does this through the baptism that he receives from John in preparation for his mission

   2. Jesus takes man's sins upon himself and places himself in solidarity with sinners

   3. Relationship of Jesus' baptism to his Cross

B. Jesus' baptism in the Church's liturgy and iconography

   1. Connection of Jesus' baptism with Epiphany in the Eastern Church's liturgy

   2. Icons connect Jesus' baptism in the water of the Jordan, in solidarity with sinners, with Jesus' harrowing of hell and conquering of the devil

C. The Lamb of God

    1. Suffering Servant of Isaiah 53, who dies for the redemption of all

    2. New Passover: liberation from death, new life in the Promised Land—not solely for Israel but for the whole world

D. The Son, the Spirit, and the Father

    1. Heaven is opened by Jesus' baptism, through his communion with the Father

    2. The Father announces Jesus' identity, and the dove (the Holy Spirit) descends upon Jesus—union with Jesus opens the Trinitarian life to us

Questions for Understanding

1. What is the significance that Benedict points out in the precise historical data given by Saint Luke to mark out the beginning of John the Baptist's life and the baptism of Jesus (pp. 10–12)?

2. What is the reason Benedict gives for the Gospel of Luke mentioning Jesus along with the Roman Caesars (pp. 11–12)?

3. What are the differences between the baptism offered by John and the religious ablutions of other Jewish practices and sects (p. 14)? How does John's role as the "forerunner" to Christ shed light on these differences (pp. 15–16)?

4. Why does Jesus ask to be baptized by John? What does it mean that Jesus is baptized to "fulfil all righteousness"? How does his baptism look forward to the Passion (pp. 16–18)?

5. Why does John call Jesus "the Lamb of God"? What ideas or practices from the Old Testament does this phrase recall (pp. 20–22)?

6. Why do the heavens open after Jesus' baptism (pp. 23–24)?

Questions for Application

1. How is baptism like a new exodus? What does it do for each believer?

2. If Christian baptism is done in imitation of Christ's baptism, what is imitated? How does Christ's baptism shed light on our own? Given what Benedict says that Christ's baptism points toward, does our baptism point toward the same thing?

3. Benedict tells us that Israel's vocation was not just for itself, but also for the whole world. He also says that Jesus' mission was for both Israel and the whole world. What does this mean for the vocation of a Christian?

4. What does it mean for me that Jesus is, as Saint Augustine says, more intimate to us than we are to our own selves? How should that influence my life? What does it mean that Pope Benedict uses these words of Augustine in the context of Jesus' baptism (p. 24)?

Terms

Augustus, 11	Saint Cyril of Jerusalem, 19
Pontius Pilate, 11	Saint John Chrysostom, 19
Zealots, 12	Paul Evdokimov, 19
Pharisees, 13	recapitulate, 20
Torah, 13	*Inferno*, 20
Sadducees, 13	Joachim Jeremias, 21
Qumran, 13	Passover, 21
Essenes, 13	Wholly Other, 24
Joachim Gnilka, 15	Saint Augustine, 24

Notes

CHAPTER TWO

The Temptations of Jesus

Summary

The temptations of Jesus are fundamentally about idolatry and about who God is. Under different forms, the devil tempts Jesus to subject the Father to judgment and to provide proof of his own divinity according to human standards. Jesus repeats or "recapitulates" (see glossary entry for "recapitulate") mankind's entire history of temptations, living through them just as men and women throughout time have had to do.

In his role as the new Adam, the Founder of a new kind of humanity, Jesus is tempted in the desert, whereas Adam was tempted in the garden. By remaining faithful through his temptations, Jesus shows that he can redeem us from the sin of Adam.

The first temptation of Jesus, to satisfy his hunger by changing stones into bread, demands that God do away with human suffering. In this temptation, hunger symbolizes all of our physical needs and the physical evils we experience. As the Son of God, Jesus, if he wished, could satisfy man's physical needs and do away with all the physical evils experienced by mankind throughout the ages, but this is not his mission. His mission is to point the way to the heavenly Kingdom, not to make sure that all earthly evils are overcome on earth. When Jesus miraculously tends to the needs of the body by feedings and healings, these signs point to the heavenly Kingdom and indicate who Jesus is.

The second temptation is for Jesus to cast himself from a height so that God will send angels to catch him. This temptation is for Jesus to submit to human requirements for certainty—in other words, to have faith on our terms, not on God's. The devil suggests that Jesus force God's hand by making the Father prove that he will care for Jesus when he is in physical danger. This would reverse the proper relationship between God and man, making God man's servant and undermining faith in God's benevolence in favor of human tests. To test God would be to say to God that man is his superior and has the right to sit in judgment over him. The second temptation involves a dispute between Jesus and the devil about the correct way to read the Scriptures. Jesus' answer, "Again it is written, 'You shall not tempt the Lord your

God'" (Mt 4:7), indicates that only the one who knows God intimately will be able to learn from the Scriptures, again pointing to the importance of faith.

The third temptation is to rule the kingdoms of the world. The devil offers Jesus the opportunity to unite all kingdoms in peace and unity, and so to abandon his message of sacrifice, humility, and self-emptying love. In this way, Jesus would grasp the glory and praise from men that he deserves as the Son of God. But Jesus has not come to carve out an earthly paradise; he has come to bring God to man and so to enable the right worship by which God is truly honored and man is really brought to happiness. Through the fulfillment of the mission the Father has given to him, Jesus wins the only glory that matters: glory from the Father, who desires the peace that can only be found in the eternal Kingdom of heaven, not in the earthly kingdoms that men build.

Outline

I. The Messiah and temptations

A. Jesus' solidarity with human struggles and his "recapitulation" (in his own life) of the history of suffering: the temptations are part of Jesus' *entire* life

B. Reversing the curse of Adam: creation must again become a garden rather than a desert

C. Adam's sin consists in succumbing to the temptation to make God secondary

D. Jesus' forty days of fasting, in the context of Old Testament parallels

  1. The Israelites' forty years' wandering in the desert (Jesus provides a new Exodus)

  2. Moses' forty days on Mount Sinai (Jesus provides a new Law)

  3. The Fathers of the Church on the cosmological symbolism of the number 40 (4×10) (Jesus provides a new creation)

II. The three temptations

A. The first temptation: "If you are the Son of God, command these stones to become loaves of bread" (Mt 4:3)

  1. The devil's demand for proof regarding Jesus' identity; similar to demand for God to prove his existence

  2. The devil's demand for Jesus to envision his mission in terms of a social gospel, feeding the poor (solving world hunger); similar to efforts to reduce the Church's mission to social work

    a. Jesus' feeding miracles (e.g., multiplication of the loaves) show his concern for hungry human beings

    b. The feeding miracles show that we should seek God's Word, trust God for sustenance, and share with each other

    c. The Eucharist

  3. Jesus responds to the devil by quoting Deuteronomy 8:3: "[M]an does not live by bread alone, but . . . by everything that proceeds out of the mouth of the LORD"

  4. Pope Benedict's critique of modern Western material assistance to poor countries, which ignores the spiritual dimension

  5. How to find God: obedience to God's Word

B. The second temptation: "If you are the Son of God, throw yourself down; for it is written, 'He will give his angels charge of you' " (Mt 4:6)

  1. The devil tempts Jesus by quoting from Psalm 91; the devil has the skills of a theologian—Vladimir Soloviev's story of the devil as a great Bible scholar

  2. God speaks through the Bible, and true biblical scholars will recognize God speaking; scholarship about the Bible is ultimately determined by who one thinks Jesus is

  3. Jesus responds to the devil by quoting Deuteronomy 6:16: "You shall not put the LORD your God to the test"—God cannot be found by empirical tests

  4. Psalm 91: God gives spiritual refuge to those who obey his will, even in the midst of suffering and personal risk

C. The third temptation: "All these I will give you, if you will fall down and worship me" (Mt 4:9)

  1. Authority on earth is never lasting or unambiguously good; authority on earth is good when it possesses God's blessing

  2. Jesus' authority in heaven and on earth comes through his Cross and Resurrection, therefore Christ's Kingdom is not a political kingdom in the sense of earthly and military power—Christ's Kingdom does not depend upon any earthly form of political power

  3. Barabbas, who was released instead of Jesus, sought to achieve the messianic age through military conquest; Jesus is Barabbas' opposite

  4. A choice between worldly power (worldly well-being) and the Cross: Jesus offers us not worldly prosperity, but God, who is the true good of man

  5. Jesus responds to the devil by quoting Deuteronomy 6:13: "You shall worship the Lord your God and him only shall you serve" (as cited in Mt 4:10)

  6. Jesus is the true mediator between heaven and earth

Questions for Understanding

1. What connection does Benedict draw out between Jesus' anointing and his temptations (pp. 25–26)?

2. How do Jesus' temptations in the desert mirror Adam's deeds in the garden (p. 27)?

3. What is at the heart of Jesus' temptations, according to Benedict (pp. 28–29)?

4. What is at the root of the first temptation, according to Benedict (p. 30)? In linking the first temptation with the miracle of the loaves and the Eucharistic Last Supper, what is Benedict saying about Jesus' mission as Redeemer (pp. 32–33)? What is he saying about the purpose of the miracles Jesus performs?

5. What is the significance of the devil's citation of Scripture in the second temptation? What is the scriptural debate really about, according to Benedict (pp. 35–36)?

6. What is at stake in our demands that God prove himself? What does Benedict say we are doing when we make these demands (p. 37)?

7. What does Benedict say about the relationship between heavenly and earthly power? Why? Why does Jesus have both heavenly and earthly power (p. 39)?

8. What is the difference between the power the devil offers and the power that Jesus claims he himself has (p. 39)? How is this difference illuminated by the choice between Barabbas and Jesus (pp. 40–41)? Why is it dangerous to expect Jesus or the Church to make the world more peaceful and prosperous (pp. 42–44)?

9. What has Jesus brought, if not universal earthly peace and prosperity? Why is this important (p. 44)?

Questions for Application

1. How are the temptations I experience illusions of a better way? How can I be more aware of God's reality, the falseness of a life without God, and his commands in the face of my temptations?

2. Do I sometimes require God to prove himself on my own terms? How? Would such a proof really be good for me? Give examples from the Gospels that might help shed light on this question.

3. What role do conversion and obedience play in understanding God's reality? Have I had a "conversion experience"? How did it change how I thought about

God? Do I seek to deepen my conversion constantly so that I can know and love God better?

4. What does the devil's quotation of Scripture teach me about how to read the Bible? Clearly, the devil can cite "chapter and verse". What brings true knowledge of Scripture, if not solely the mastery of texts which the devil displays?

5. In my daily life, do I choose Barabbas or Jesus? Do I tend toward the kind of power the devil offers or the power Jesus has? Do I make earthly peace, prosperity, and success the standard for authentic faith?

Terms

Notes

CHAPTER THREE

The Gospel of the Kingdom of God

Summary

The core of Jesus' message is the coming of the Kingdom of God in history with the coming of Christ. It is this to which the Church witnesses in her preaching about Jesus. Unlike the pretensions of the Roman emperors to divinity and their false claims to bring peace to men, Jesus' actions point to his divinity and offer true peace to men. This peace is not to be found in a kingdom ruled by earthly might, but in God's heavenly Kingdom, which is ruled by God in love.

Jesus does more than teach about the Kingdom of God. Christ (the messenger) and the message he brings are the same: he preaches about the Kingdom of God and he himself is the Kingdom of God. Perfect communion with Jesus, who is in perfect communion with the Father, brings true peace.

In the last few centuries many distortions have crept into the way some theologians understand the Kingdom of God. These distortions remove God from the center of the Kingdom of God and replace him with man. As a result, human efforts, without reference to God, are now thought to build the Kingdom of God, which consists in earthly peace, justice, and environmental responsibility.

Benedict argues that a correct Christ-centered (christocentric) and God-centered (theocentric) understanding of the Kingdom of God avoids the separation of ethics and grace, a separation that is at the heart of this false, human-centered conception of the Kingdom. The Kingdom of God grows in history and reaches completion in eternity; its growth involves human works empowered by grace, but only by *grace*—God's gift of his life and power—is man capable of building the true Kingdom of God. God must remain at the center of our understanding of the Kingdom of God.

Outline

I. The meaning of the word *evangelium*

A. A message issued by a Roman emperor, "salvific" news for the world

B. The *evangelium*, or "Gospel", is truly what the Roman emperors falsely claimed their messages were

C. A message issued about the true kingdom, the Kingdom of God

D. Modernist biblical scholar Albert Loisy's claim that Jesus preached the arrival of the Kingdom, but instead the Church arrived

E. What is the relationship between the Church and the Kingdom, and, therefore, more fundamentally between Christ and the Kingdom?

II. The meaning of "Kingdom"

A. Views of "Kingdom" in the history of the Church
   1. Jesus himself is the Kingdom
   2. The Kingdom of God is the holy soul (Origen of Alexandria)
   3. The Kingdom of God is related closely to the Church

B. View of "Kingdom" in twentieth-century liberal Protestant theology
   1. Adolf von Harnack: Jesus focused on the value of the individual person over the People of God and emphasized works of love over priestly worship
   2. Johannes Weiss and Albert Schweitzer: Jesus was an eschatological prophet, proclaiming the restoration of Israel (inbreaking of the new creation)

C. View of "Kingdom" in contemporary Catholic theology
   1. Neither "ecclesiocentrism" nor "Christocentrism" nor "theocentrism", but rather Jesus' proclamation of an ecologically responsible, peaceful, and just world ("regnocentrism")
   2. The Kingdom as the pinnacle of human cultural-political-ecological achievement, born out of the interplay of the various religions
   3. Man, not God, is the center of this Kingdom

III. Kingdom of *God*

A. Matthew's Gospel uses the phrase "kingdom of heavens", but this means Kingdom of God

B. Both the Hebrew and the Greek words for "kingdom" indicate the king's active sovereignty, not merely a future kingdom

C. Jesus' proclamation of the Kingdom is a proclamation of the living God's existence and action in the world as its King or Lord

IV. Jesus' preaching of the Kingdom

   A. Old Testament antecedents

      1. First, the proclamation of God's kingship celebrated his sovereignty over the whole world

      2. After the Exile in 587 B.C., the proclamation of God's kingship focused on God's *return* as King

      3. In first-century Judaism, prayer (especially liturgical prayer) was seen as a participation in, and making present of, God's lordship/kingship

   B. Jesus' parables on the growth of the Kingdom

   C. The Kingdom is close to us because the Kingdom is Jesus; we thrive when we recognize our need for Jesus/God

Questions for Understanding

1. The Roman emperors used the word *evangelium*, which the Gospel writers adapted for their purposes. What is the significance of this move (pp. 46–47)?

2. How does Benedict say we are to understand the fact that Christ's preaching before Easter centered on the Kingdom of God, while the apostles' preaching after Easter focused on Christ (pp. 48–49)?

3. What are the three ways the Church Fathers understood "Kingdom of God" (pp. 49–50)? How might they be related? How does more recent scholarship, both Protestant and Catholic, understand "the Kingdom of God" (pp. 51–54)? What is wrong with the vision of the Kingdom of God merely as the work of religion and the ushering in of peace and justice on earth (pp. 54–55)?

4. What is the relationship between prayer and the Kingdom of God (pp. 57–58)?

5. What is the relationship between grace and ethics that Pope Benedict mentions? How is this related to the discussion of the Kingdom of God and the erroneous claims about the Kingdom that Benedict mentions as present in theology today (pp. 61–62)?

Questions for Application

1. How does the Kingdom of God grow in my soul? What role does Christ have? The Church?

2. How does my own prayer extend the lordship of God (pp. 57–59)? What does this say about the role of God in my prayers (pp. 61–62)? How can the story of the

prayers of the tax collector and the Pharisee provide understanding? What, then, should be the character of my prayers?

3. When I pray or go to Mass, is it more important to me what I bring to prayer, the sacrament, and the liturgy, or what I receive from God through prayer, the sacrament, and the liturgy?

Terms

evangelium, 47
Rudolf Bultmann, 48
Alfred Loisy, 48
autobasileia, 49
Patrologia Graeca, 50
K. L. Schmidt, 52
Martin Heidegger, 53
Jürgen Moltmann, 53
Ernst Bloch, 53

ecclesiocentrism, 53
Christocentrism, 53
theocentrism, 53
regnocentrism, 53
Peter Stuhlmacher, 55
YHWH, 56
rabbinic literature, 57
Shema Israel, 57

Notes

The Sermon on the Mount

Summary

The Sermon on the Mount marks out Jesus as the New Moses. As Moses was the teacher of Israel, so Jesus is the teacher of a renewed Israel; as Moses gave Israel God's Law, or Torah, so Jesus gives a new Law in the Sermon on the Mount, only the new Torah is for the whole world. The Law that Jesus gives is not opposed to the Law of Moses but presupposes it, deepens it, and makes it universal—for everyone for all time, not simply for Israel. In this way, Jesus can be seen as the greater Moses, who extends God's covenant to all the world.

Benedict examines three main things in his discussion of the Sermon on the Mount, two of which he discusses in chapter four and the third which he discusses in chapter five. The two main elements of chapter four are the Beatitudes and the new Law of Jesus.

The Beatitudes are central to the Sermon on the Mount. They do not overturn the Ten Commandments of the Old Testament but repeat them and deepen how they are to be lived. The Beatitudes are words of promise, criteria for discernment, and directions for right living. They promise that Christ's way of life leads to true happiness—beatitude or blessedness. They sum up the paradoxes at the heart of Christ's life and the life of his disciples: humility, love, and self-emptying suffering for others lead to happiness. The saints are constant reminders that Christian discipleship brings happiness.

Matthew lists eight Beatitudes. The first Beatitude, "Blessed are the poor in spirit, for theirs is the kingdom of heaven", refers not only to the materially poor, but to those who humbly recognize their need for God. The third Beatitude, "Blessed are the meek, for they shall inherit the earth", is linked to the first, for the meek are the poor in spirit. Benedict especially offers Moses and Jesus as examples of meekness. To "inherit the earth" means primarily to inherit a place to worship rightly: the Promised Land of Israel in the Old Testament and the Church in the New, both pointing to heaven.

The seventh Beatitude, "Blessed are the peacemakers, for they shall be called sons of God", refers to peace with God, which entails obedience to him. Obedience to God is what marks a son of God. The second Beatitude, "Blessed are those who mourn, for they shall be comforted", refers to those who mourn for sin. This mourning opens the way for conversion and hope and is contrasted with the evil mourning of despair.

The eighth Beatitude, "Blessed are those who are persecuted for righteousness' sake, for theirs is the kingdom of heaven", is linked to the seventh since those who identify sins, both in themselves and in others, will be persecuted. Christ and his Church will always be persecuted for witnessing against sin. Christ's persecution ended in death, but he rose again; the persecuted Church will likewise follow her master.

The fourth Beatitude, "Blessed are those who hunger and thirst for righteousness, for they shall be satisfied", promises that those who seek after God, for the truly transcendent, will find happiness and peace. Only God can satisfy man. The sixth Beatitude, "Blessed are the pure in heart, for they shall see God", identifies purity as the harmony of body and soul, and the obedience of the entire man, body and soul, to God. The pure in heart obeys God's commands and follows Christ, which grants to the man what he most wants: to see God.

Throughout the sermon, Jesus speaks in such a way as to claim the authority of God. He makes himself the touchstone of the new Law, by claiming lordship over the Sabbath, replacing the Temple and Torah with himself, and making fidelity to the covenant consist in following him. On these points Benedict discusses Rabbi Jacob Neusner's book about Jesus. He agrees with Neusner that the Person of Christ is ultimately where Jews and Christians diverge, with Christians seeing Jesus as occupying the place of God and founding a new, universal community out of the old Israel, upon himself.

Jesus teaches that the state of perfection, of complete holiness and commitment to God, now consists in following him, of being his disciple. If Jesus were not divine, his claim would be horrifying. Benedict nevertheless contends that those who know who Jesus is, who know him as the Son of Man, are able to see that he fulfills and does not abolish the faith and way of life of the people of Israel. In allowing non-Israelites to share in the promise, Jesus fulfills Israel's vocation to be a "light to the nations", to the Gentiles (Is 42:6). Everyone who hears Jesus and follows him can be his disciple. The New Moses is therefore the Greater Moses; he is the Messiah.

Outline

I. Jesus, the Greater Moses

    A. Jesus fulfills Deuteronomy's promises and the Law

    B. Seated on the mountain, Jesus teaches the people as the Greater Moses

    C. Just as Moses mediates between the people and God, so does Jesus by his Cross—but in Jesus God enters into man's condition

    D. Moses delivers the Torah after communing with God at the top of Mount Sinai; Jesus delivers the New Law in communion with his Father

E. Jesus' New Law calls the whole world, not just Israel, to obedience

F. Jesus' New Law deepens, but does not repudiate, the Decalogue

II. The Beatitudes

A. What are the Beatitudes?

1. Promises of blessing, both now and eternally, for those who trust the Lord

2. Directions for finding the true path of holiness

3. Jesus' disciples are described in the Beatitudes

4. Jesus turns the world's standards for success upside-down

5. The Beatitudes describe Jesus himself

B. "Blessed are the poor in spirit, for theirs is the kingdom of heaven" (first)

1. The materially poor are often spiritually "poor" in the sense of trusting absolutely in God rather than in themselves

2. Voluntary poverty of Christian ascetics (e.g., Saint Francis)

C. "Blessed are the meek, for they shall inherit the earth" (third)

1. The "meek" are God's poor (including, e.g., Moses—not simply the materially poor)

2. Jesus' meekness, his self-giving love and humility, and his lordship

3. The "earth" is the land, the Promised Land understood as the land where the true God is worshipped

4. The Eucharist as foreshadowing this inheritance

D. "Blessed are the peacemakers, for they shall be called sons of God" (seventh)

1. Jesus truly embodies what was foreshadowed by David's son Solomon, who reigned in peace

2. Without reconciliation with God (true inner peace), there will be violence in the world

E. "Blessed are those who mourn, for they shall be comforted" (second)

1. Mourning for our sins, or for the sins of our country (in passive resistance), prompts conversion and renewal

2. The Virgin Mary and John at the foot of the Cross

F. "Blessed are those who are persecuted for righteousness' sake, for theirs is the kingdom of heaven" (eighth)

1. Those who "mourn" their own sins and those of the world suffer persecution for identifying sinful practices

    2. A persecuted Church, both under the Roman Empire and insofar as the Church is a sign of contradiction to the world's values

    3. Christ is persecuted and raised from the dead

G. "Blessed are those who hunger and thirst for righteousness, for they shall be satisfied" (fourth)

    1. Those who seek something greater, true holiness, rather than giving in to convention

    2. The path that unites to Jesus even those who do not consciously know him

H. "Blessed are the pure in heart, for they shall see God" (sixth)

    1. Purity of the unified person, body and soul—embodied holiness, which requires obedience to the content of the Decalogue

    2. Purity of heart results from truly following Christ in love, through man's relationship with Christ in service and obedience to him

I. Are the Beatitudes the true path of human happiness?

    1. The Gospel of Luke lists certain false paths, which threaten to entice us to cleave to this world

    2. Friedrich Nietzsche's critique of the ethics of the Beatitudes: Nietzsche desires this kingdom of earth, not the Kingdom of heaven—Pope Benedict shows how this attitude leads to oppression (via worship of Mammon)

    3. God, not autonomy or the pretense of self-sufficiency, makes man happy

III. The Torah of the Messiah

A. "You have heard that it was said . . . but I say to you"

    1. The Law of Christ is freedom, because it consists in being led by the Spirit of God, and it therefore fulfills the Law of Moses

    2. No longer simply a Law for Israel

    3. Jacob Neusner's *A Rabbi Talks with Jesus* argues that Jesus is mistaken to restructure the content of the Torah around following Jesus, because Jesus claims the place of God—Pope Benedict devotes the remainder of the chapter to dialoguing with Neusner

B. The dispute concerning the Sabbath

    1. Neusner and Pope Benedict agree that Jesus is not a liberal rabbi who simply dismisses the Torah as legalistic

    2. According to Neusner, Jesus claims to replace the Temple, the Torah, and the Sabbath with himself, and Jesus also restructures the people

of Israel around himself—Pope Benedict shows how this restructured Sabbath and new Israel is found in the Church's Eucharist

C. The Fourth Commandment: the family, the people, and the community of Jesus' disciples

1. According to Neusner, Jesus' view that his family consists in his disciples, not in his relatives according to the flesh, undermines the continuity of God's people through the generations and tends toward individualism—Pope Benedict shows that Jesus' family, centered upon the bond of communion with the Son through the spirit of holiness, draws the nations into relationship with the God of Israel, a relationship marked by obedient freedom

2. Pope Benedict emphasizes the difference between fulfillment and negation of the Law of Moses: Christ fulfills, he does not negate

3. Jesus can only transcend and fulfill the Law of Moses because Jesus possesses divine authority as the Son of God

D. Compromise and prophetic radicalism

1. Would the ethics of the Sermon on the Mount, if followed, destroy the social order because of their alleged lack of realism (e.g., love of enemy, no divorce)?

    a. Distinguishes between apodictic law (divine commands, unchangeable) and casuistic law (very specific legal issues, open to development)

    b. Love of God and love of neighbor cannot be compromised—this constitutes the radical character of the Sermon on the Mount

2. Jesus realistically allows prudence to govern the judicial and social laws of nations, even as he insists upon radical love of God and love of neighbor

Questions for Understanding

1. What is the significance of the setting of the Sermon on the Mount (pp. 66–67)?

2. How is Christ's life necessary for understanding the Beatitudes (p. 74)?

3. How does Benedict connect meekness, worship, obedience to God, and possession of the land (pp. 80–83)? In light of these connections, how are we to understand the universality of Christ's message (p. 84)?

4. How does mourning set limits to evil (pp. 87–88)? What is the difference between the mourning of Judas and of Peter (p. 86)? How can we understand mourning better at the foot of the Cross (p. 87)?

5. How are faith and righteousness related (p. 89)?

6. How is Christology at the heart of the Sermon on the Mount?

7. What does Benedict mean when he speaks of the heart? How are man's mind, will, and passions, his body and soul, all at work together in seeing God (pp. 92–94)?

8. What are the conditions Benedict mentions for the heart's purification (p. 94)? What role do humility and love have to play (p. 95)?

9. What is the difference between the hunger and thirst for righteousness and the this-worldly lust for life Benedict presents in Nietzsche's thought (pp. 97–99)? What are the consequences of each way of life? How might the Christian and the disciple of Nietzsche view love differently? Humility? Self-sacrifice?

10. How are freedom and law related in the "law of Christ" (Gal 6:2)? Why does Benedict say that the Ten Commandments, and by extension the Old Testament, is presupposed and fulfilled in the Torah of the Messiah (pp. 99–100)?

11. What is the reason for the alarm of Jesus' audience to the Sermon on the Mount (pp. 102–3)? What is the fundamental difference that Rabbi Jacob Neusner draws out between the Christian and Jewish faiths (p. 105)? Why does Neusner find this so disturbing (p. 106)?

12. What is the root of the Sabbath dispute? What is really at stake? What do Benedict and Neusner say about the interpretation of Jesus as a forerunner of liberal Christianity, preaching freedom to narrow-minded legalism? What would it mean for Jesus to be Lord of the Sabbath (pp. 107–11)?

13. Why is Neusner concerned that Jesus' Sabbath teaching corrodes the People of God? What does Benedict say about the Christian Lord's Day in this regard (pp. 111–12)?

14. Why does Benedict say that the broadening of Israel into the Church is connected with Jesus' claim to divinity? What does Benedict point to in Israel's own vocation that justifies Christ's universalization of Israel into the Church? How is this related to the conditions of membership in Israel and in the Church, respectively (pp. 116–17)? In light of this, what does Benedict say was at stake in Saint Paul's dispute with the "Judaizers" (pp. 121–22)?

15. What are the enormous implications of the universalization Christ brings— which is based on faith and not common descent or any particular national law— for the political order (p. 122)?

16. What are the differences Benedict cites between casuistic law and apodictic law (pp. 123–25)? What is their relationship in the Old Testament (pp. 125–26)? How does this difference provide a way to give the criteria for building up social and political communities? What does Benedict say about Christian social teaching in this context (pp. 126–27)?

Questions for Application

1. Have I ever experienced joy or consolation from my own suffering? If yes, what allows this? If no, how might meditation on the Cross and the Beatitudes help to transform my experience of suffering? How can suffering and poverty lead me closer to God?

2. How can the saints enable me to understand the Scriptures (p. 78)?

3. Reflect on a time when you knew yourself to be particularly obedient to God and at peace. How did your body and soul work together? How did your mind, will, and passions interact? What does Benedict say about the priority of obedience to God? How is the peace of body and soul, mind, will, and passions working together, achieved? What do I need to do to achieve this peace?

4. Do I ever ignore my own hunger and thirst for righteousness out of a lust for some worldly good? How can the Beatitudes help counteract this temptation?

5. How do I use the Lord's Day? Is it a day of rest in Christ? What kind of freedom do I practice on Sundays?

6. How would my life be different if Christ had not liberated politics from its theocratic tendencies? What would both worship and civic life be like? How does the genuine secularity of the state that Jesus allows free me to worship well? How does it free me to be a better citizen? How is secularity of the state different from secularism (pp. 126–27)?

Terms

Notes

CHAPTER FIVE

The Lord's Prayer

Summary

We cannot pray as we ought, according to Benedict XVI, so God graciously provides the words for our prayer. Normally, our thinking precedes our speaking. Yet in the Psalms, the liturgy, and the Lord's Prayer, God calls us to take his words as our starting point and standard so that our thoughts and therefore our actions are conformed to his will for us. Because this prayer is Jesus' prayer, when we pray it we enter into Jesus' deep communion with the Father.

There are seven petitions in the Lord's Prayer: three "thou" petitions and four petitions asking God to help our needs and desires. This division corresponds to the two tablets of the Ten Commandments and the two parts of the Great Commandment (Mt 22:37–40) to love God and neighbor. The prayer is directed to the Father, who is addressed in the first person plural, "our" Father, since God is Father of all his children by virtue of communion with Christ our brother. The first petition, "Hallowed be thy name", reminds us that God has given his name for a reason—to establish a relationship with us—and therefore his name should not be abused. The second petition, "Thy kingdom come", orders all our priorities so that God comes first. The third petition, "Thy will be done on earth as it is in heaven", aligns our wills with what God wills for us.

The fourth petition, "Give us this day our daily bread", reminds us that every good thing comes from God. This petition exhorts us to draw close to Jesus in the Eucharist. The fifth petition, "And forgive us our trespasses, as we forgive those who trespass against us", teaches us that receiving forgiveness and forgiving are intimately united. The sixth petition, "And lead us not into temptation", tells us that it is proper to ask God not to test us beyond our strength, while acknowledging that the encounter with evil is necessary for us to grow in holiness. The final petition, "But deliver us from evil", asks God to free us from the temptation to despair and to place our trust in things or in people who are not God, rather than in God.

Outline

I. True and false prayer

    A. False prayer: showing off, chatter

    B. True prayer: personal intimacy, interior recollection

    C. Prayer both follows upon and nourishes our communion with God

    D. Formulaic prayers teach us how to pray, a lesson that is necessary due to the greatness and mysteriousness of God

II. Jesus' own prayer as the context for ours

    A. The Our Father is found in Luke's Gospel in the context of Jesus' prayer

    B. We can learn from the Our Father how to enter into the dialogue of the incarnate Son with his Father through the Holy Spirit—in this way we deepen our participation in God's Trinitarian life

    C. The first three petitions have to do with love of God; the following four involve love of neighbor/self—similar to the Decalogue's structure

    D. When we begin with the primacy of God, we are open to conversion of heart and mind

III. Our Father who art in heaven

    A. Jesus teaches us the divine Father's goodness and love

        1. The Father's gift to us, in Christ and through the Holy Spirit, is God himself—which is what we really need

        2. In the Son's self-giving love, we learn about the Father

    B. The Father is Father as Creator, and also as Father of his only Son. In the first way we are already in God's image; but God calls us to be like his full Image, the Son, and thus to be sons in the Son

    C. The Bible at times describes God's love as maternal, but the Bible does not describe God as Mother, probably because mother-deities imply pantheism rather than creation

    D. In praying to "our" Father, we pray with the whole Church, the whole family of God, rather than as isolated monads

IV. Hallowed be thy name

    A. The name of God: "I am who I am"—this indicates that God is sheer "being", sheer "is"

B. God's name is transcendent and mysterious, but in Christ God has manifested his "name" or divine identity in a fully human fashion

C. When we use the name of God for selfish purposes, we distort who he is and fail to reverence his name

V. Thy Kingdom come

A. The Kingdom of God is the domain of righteousness

B. If we desire the onset of God's Kingdom, we must give ourselves entirely to God rather than seek to bring God's Kingdom about from our own resources

VI. Thy will be done on earth as it is in heaven

A. The Decalogue, as deepened by the Sermon on the Mount, reveals God's will

B. Jesus is "heaven" because he is fully transparent to God's will—we must become like him

VII. Give us this day our daily bread

A. We should pray for our daily needs and for the needs of others, and our actions should help others meet their needs

B. Voluntary poverty in the Church bears radical witness to our need for daily dependence on God for basic needs

C. The Greek word *epiousios*, translated "daily", is otherwise unknown—it may also have Eucharistic dimensions, beyond material bread

D. The bread that most fully binds us together, as "our" daily bread, is the Eucharist

VIII. And forgive us our trespasses, as we forgive those who trespass against us

A. God's forgiveness outpaces ours; God bears all our sins in Christ Jesus

B. Forgiveness is costly and difficult

C. To appreciate forgiveness, including the forgiveness of all through the expiatory sacrifice of one man, we need to recognize how interconnected all human beings are

D. We find power to forgive others in the transformative forgiveness that Christ accomplished for us

IX. And lead us not into temptation

A. God permits that we endure temptations, but he does not tempt us to sin

B. In overcoming temptations and enduring trials, we are purified and become spiritually stronger—but we must pray that God not allow us to face temptations and trials that we cannot bear, so that we do not fall

C. By allowing the devil to tempt us, God counters our tendency to imagine that we are self-sufficient and thereby strengthens us in Christ-like self-giving, as exemplified by the saints who have overcome temptations and trials

X. But deliver us from evil

A. "Evil" could also be translated "the evil one"; either way, it is the same deliverance we are seeking

B. So long as we retain our hold on God, we have not been conquered by evil; God is the Good who is the key to our happiness, and without him we are miserable

C. In asking to be delivered from evil, we are also asking to be delivered from difficult and almost unbearable tribulations that we face in our lives, and that threaten to divert us from union with God

Questions for Understanding

1. What does Benedict say is the root reason that prayer is important for us? Why is discretion in prayer important? How is proper discretion in prayer compatible with communal prayer? What is meant by "pray without ceasing" (pp. 128–30)?

2. What is the significance of God providing our prayer? How is this different from our usual experience of thinking and speaking? Why is this necessary (pp. 130–31)? How does this find expression in authentic Christian mysticism (pp. 131–32)?

3. What is the relationship Benedict draws out between the Lord's Prayer, the two tablets of the Decalogue (Ten Commandments) and the Great Commandment (Mt 22:37–40) to love God and neighbor (p. 134)?

4. What does "Father" mean for Jesus (p. 136)? What does it mean that we say "our Father" and not "my Father"?

5. What does it mean that we are not complete children of God from the outset? What does this imply about the spiritual life? What is the function of prayer for us, who are not perfect children of God from the outset (p. 138)?

6. What does it mean that "mother" is an image but not a title for God (pp. 139–40)?

7. What is a name? What does the giving of a name imply? How was the giving of the name of God a foreshadowing of the Incarnation? How is the burning bush in Exodus completed at the burning bush of the Cross? Why does Benedict ultimately say that the petition to keep God's name holy is necessary (pp. 142–45)?

8. How does earth become heaven (pp. 147–48)? What is Jesus' role in bringing this about? How does the petition "Thy will be done, on earth as it is in heaven" help?

9. If Jesus tells us not to worry about providing food for ourselves (Mt 6:25), why does he include the petition "Give us this day our daily bread" in the Lord's Prayer (pp. 150–51)? What is the implication about those who must ask for bread? Why do we ask for "our" bread and not "my" bread (pp. 151–52)? How is this petition related to the Eucharist (pp. 154–57)?

10. What does Benedict say about who must initiate forgiveness? Why (p. 158)? How does God's action in history shed light on this (p. 159)? What are our age's particular obstacles to understanding divine forgiveness (pp. 159–60)? How is the petition "Forgive us our trespasses" related to Christ (p. 160)?

11. Does God really tempt man to sin (pp. 160–61)? How are we to understand the petition "lead us not into temptation" (p. 163)?

12. What is the "evil" mentioned in the Lord's Prayer from which we need to be delivered (pp. 165–66)? How does the last petition of the Lord's Prayer, "deliver us from evil", lead back to the first, "Thy kingdom come" (p. 167)?

Questions for Application

1. What role does prayer play in my life? Is it my soul's bedrock? Do I have recourse to prayer constantly? Which insights into the Lord's Prayer that Benedict offers can help me to make prayer my foundation and to pray unceasingly?

2. Do I allow the prayers that God has given the Church—the liturgy, the Psalms, the Lord's Prayer—to take me up and conform me to them, or do I often or sometimes attempt to substitute my own voice for them? Do I try to receive them graciously, or do I attempt to adapt them to my own desires and to what I think they should be?

3. Do I allow prayer to correct my desires? Do I allow prayer to teach me if my desires are rightly ordered?

4. Reflect on the questions Benedict asks at the end of the section "Hallowed Be Thy Name" (p. 145).

5. How does the petition "Thy Kingdom come" order your priorities in life? Give concrete examples. Give examples of other biblical figures from the Old and New Testament who put God's Kingdom first. How does God treat them? How can I emulate these figures in my own life?

6. Reflect on Jesus' agony in the garden. How does he align his will with the Father's? How do I? How can I learn from Jesus to align my will with the Father's?

7. Do I attempt to seek out one who has offended me in order to offer forgiveness, or do I hold myself back, making him come to me? When I am approached by someone whom I have offended offering forgiveness, how do I react?

8. Do I regard the encounter with evil as an opportunity to grow in holiness? Do I pray for God not to test me beyond my strength?

Terms

Saint Benedict, 131	*epiousios*, 153
Rule of Saint Benedict, 131	Saint Jerome's Vulgate, 154
Saint Cyprian, 131	*supersubstantialis*, 154
Father Peter-Hans Kolvenbach, 135	Cardinal John Henry Newman,
Reinhold Schneider, 135	160
rahamim, 139	Saint Francis Xavier, 162
Martin Buber, 144	*vom Bösen*, 165

Notes

CHAPTER SIX

The Disciples

Summary

Benedict moves from the "our" of the Our Father to discuss the "we" of God's "family", showing that this family has a particular structure; it is founded upon "the Twelve", a core of Jesus' disciples whom he set apart as leaders/founders of his restored or new Israel, the Church. The number twelve is associated with the founding of the people of Israel—from the twelve tribes descended from Jacob/Israel. Benedict emphasizes that Jesus calls the disciples after spending time in prayer, signaling that Jesus chose the inner group of his intimate followers from the heart of his communion with the Father. Mark's account of the calling of the Twelve shows that the apostolic ministry is both priestly and prophetic by taking up the Old Testament language for the appointment to the priesthood and naming the apostles individually just as the Old Testament prophets were named and called individually.

Benedict observes that the apostle carries out a twofold task: remaining with Jesus and being sent out to preach. The apostles remain with Jesus in order to get to know him intimately; only by getting to know Jesus in this way will they come to recognize Jesus' oneness with the Father, which will become the bedrock for their mission to the world. Benedict mentions three primary apostolic ministries: preaching, exorcism, and healing. The apostles announce Jesus and free people from demons and sickness as signs of the Kingdom of God's presence in Jesus and of Jesus' relationship to the Father.

The apostles are extraordinarily diverse. They are all believing Jews, but among them are Zealots (Simon and Judas), who are members of a Jewish faction dedicated to the liberation of the Holy Land from Roman rule; a tax collector (Levi-Matthew) who cooperates with the occupying Roman government; fishermen (Peter, his brother Andrew, James, and John); and Greek-speaking Jews who have been assimilated into Hellenistic culture (Philip and the other Andrew). Jesus is able to bring them together in true communion, but their differences point out one of the constant challenges in the Church: diverse men are made one in Jesus Christ.

Benedict discusses the biblical significance of the numbers twelve and seventy (or seventy-two). The uniqueness of Luke's Gospel is highlighted: among the Synoptics only Luke mentions the Seventy (or Seventy-two), a larger group of Jesus' followers symbolizing the universality of Jesus' mission to all peoples. Other unique features of Luke's Gospel are discussed.

Outline

I. The calling of the Twelve

A. Jesus sought to give his family of disciples a visible structure; the Gospel of Mark depicts Jesus calling the twelve apostles on a mountain (symbolic of communion with God) and the Gospel of Luke indicates that Jesus spent the night in prayer before selecting the Twelve

B. Jesus chooses his disciples rather than his disciples choosing Jesus—God's will, not our own resources, is the foundation of our call to follow him

C. Jesus' selection of the Twelve is described by Mark in language used in the Old Testament for appointment to the priesthood, thus indicating that the disciples/apostles receive a priestly ministry. They are also named and called individually, which hearkens back to the call of the Old Testament prophets and indicates their prophetic office

D. The Twelve constitute both the restoration of Israel (of whose tribes, by the first century, only Judah fully remained), and a new Israel

E. Twelve is also a symbolic number, indicating cosmic fullness that will be attained in the Church Triumphant

F. Jesus can be seen as a new Jacob: recall that Jacob, father of the twelve tribes, dreamed of a ladder connecting heaven and earth and that Jacob later received the name Israel—Jesus, who is the mediator connecting heaven and earth, reestablishes the Twelve now as his own family

II. The mission of the Twelve

A. To be with Jesus
   1. Communion with Jesus is required to recognize who he is
   2. Communion with Jesus is necessary to carry his message to others

B. To preach
   1. The content of preaching is the Kingdom of God, God's family
   2. Not solely words, but words that convey an encounter with the Lord

C. To exorcise demons
   1. The preaching of Christ sweeps away superstitious fears and liberates the world from the proliferation of false gods

2. The preaching of Christ exorcises the poisonous spiritual climate that afflicts man

D. To heal

1. As opposed to magical healing, based on the manipulation of the forces that we fear, the apostles perform miracles of medical and, most importantly, spiritual healing

2. Miracles of healing belong within the context of uniting man to Jesus in faith

III. The identity of the Twelve

A. Each disciple is named, showing God's personal love

B. From Zealots to tax collectors: a wide variety of observant Jews

IV. Other followers of Jesus

A. The group of seventy(-two) mentioned in the Gospel of Luke symbolizes the number of the nations and also corresponds to the tradition about the translation of the Septuagint (Greek version of the Hebrew scriptures)

B. The women who followed Jesus

C. The Gospel of Luke's contribution to Christian understanding regarding the Jews

Questions for Understanding

1. What are different ways that the term "apostle" can be used (p. 169)?

2. What symbolism does the author connect with the number twelve? What connection does Benedict make between the number twelve and the priesthood (p. 171)? Between the number twelve and the prophets? How is the number twelve a symbol of Israel?

3. What is the "double assignment" that Christ gives the Twelve (p. 172)? How are the two components connected?

4. How does Benedict connect the apostles' mission to preach with that of casting out demons? How does Christianity bring with it a kind of exorcism? How is Christianity's "exorcistic" character spoken of in Ephesians 6 (pp. 173–74)?

5. How is healing linked with exorcism? In what way do exorcism and healing bring about the Kingdom of God (p. 176)?

6. Benedict mentions how in the Gospels the apostles are called by name. He also points out that there is a great variety among those who were chosen as apostles. What are some of the differences among the apostles (pp. 177–79)?

7. What does the number seventy (or seventy-two) symbolize? Where is the Old Testament basis for this symbolism? What is the legend that Benedict speaks of in relation to the number Seventy (or Seventy-two)? What is the significance of the Septuagint in leading men to Christ?

8. Benedict mentions that it is in Luke's Gospel alone that the seventy or seventy-two are mentioned. He points out other features unique in Luke's Gospel. What are some of these?

Questions for Application

1. Benedict points out that the choice of the apostles is born out of Christ's prayer and communion with the Father. There is a motto in spirituality: "to contemplate and to give to others the fruits of contemplation". How can you imitate Christ in having your work flow forth from your prayer and your relationship with him?

2. Benedict speaks of how prayer is central to the selection of the apostles and to asking God to send laborers for his vineyard (p. 170). What does this teach us about the source of vocations? About encouraging vocations?

3. In light of the "double assignment" that Jesus gives the Twelve, how can we participate in the life of the apostles by being with Jesus and bearing witness to him?

Terms

Rudolf Pesch, 173	Sons of Thunder, 178
Henri de Lubac, 173	Letter of Aristeas, 179
Heinrich Schlier, 174	

Notes

The Message of the Parables

Summary

In chapter seven, Benedict begins by speaking of the parables in general and then he highlights three particular parables in Luke's Gospel—the parable of the good Samaritan, the parable of the prodigal son, and the parable of the rich man and Lazarus. Benedict draws upon recent scholarship as well as the understanding of the Church Fathers and tradition to interpret these parables. He emphasizes that Christ himself is an important key to understanding the parables.

Benedict draws out the limits of the "liberal" approach to interpreting Jesus' parables. He criticizes the attempt to limit the parables of Jesus to one particular understanding of what makes a parable or to a parable making one "salient point". These approaches lose the richness of the parables and tend to conform them to the prejudices of the interpreter.

Jesus Christ himself and the coming of the Kingdom of God in Christ's Person are the heart of the parables, according to Benedict. The parables must be read in light of Isaiah (Is 6:9), whom Jesus quotes to explain his own use of parables (Mk 4:12), and in light of Jesus' own path to the Cross. The Isaiah passage refers to prophetic failure and rejection by Israel; the Cross is the way Jesus is rejected by Israel. But this failure of Jesus also, of course, gives proof of Christ's lordship and oneness with the Father. The Cross furnishes the means to understand the parables.

The parable of the good Samaritan (Lk 10:25–37) is about who a "neighbor" is. Benedict recalls that the common understanding of the term at the time points to a member of one's own people. The priest and the Levite, men who know the Law, both pass by the man who lies beaten and robbed at the side of the road, perhaps out of fear for their own safety. The Samaritan, however, is moved with love for the man in his plight and rescues him, entrusting him to a friendly innkeeper for his recovery. Jesus turns the question of who is one's neighbor on its head: he shows that one becomes a neighbor through love and compassion. The Church Fathers understood the injured man to be Adam, or common man, who has lost the grace he had before Original Sin and bears a wounded nature; the Samaritan is God, who has compassion on man by sending his Son to rescue him, entrusting him to the Church.

The parable of the two brothers (Lk 15:11–32), also known as the parable of the prodigal son, features a magnanimous father who gives his youngest son the freedom and resources to do whatever he wants to do. The son squanders that freedom and wastes those resources on dissolute living. Benedict points to the reading of the Church Fathers, who interpreted the parable to mean that the youngest son had ruptured his relationship with the Father on a deep, interior level because of the son's desire to live unchained from any authority. This results in his ruin and enslavement to sin rather than liberation. The son realizes his error and sin, converts, and returns to the father who, upon recognizing the son's interior conversion, welcomes him back wholeheartedly.

The Fathers read the youngest son as Adam, sinful man who has attempted to live outside of God's authority and is now in ruin and in need of repentance, and the father as welcoming the repentant sinner back and reclothing him with the grace he lost because of sin. Jesus likens himself to the father of the parable, since he too welcomes back the sinner. The implicit Christology and Trinitarian theology provide the heart of the parable. The second brother resents his younger brother's quick welcome, betraying his own secret and not-acted-upon desire to experience "freedom" apart from obedience to the father; the older brother does not recognize the grace of being always with his father. This brother represents the righteous who view their relationship with God legalistically, and who are also in need of conversion so that they will understand that the God of the Law is also the God of Love. This makes sense of the context in which Jesus tells the parable: as a response to the Pharisees' rebuke of Jesus for eating with sinners and tax collectors.

The parable of the rich man and Lazarus (Lk 16:19–31) has as its backdrop Old Testament reflection on the question of why the wicked so often prosper and the just so often suffer in earthly terms. Like the Psalms (e.g., Psalms 44 and 73), this parable reveals the unhappy circumstance of the wicked man who prospers: he cannot understand the Word of God, in which man finds his true happiness. The deeper lesson of the parable occurs in its second half, where the rich man asks Abraham for a sign that his relatives may avoid his fate. Abraham refuses, telling him that messengers from beyond the grave will not help those who have not listened to the Scriptures already. Testing God is not to be done because it misconstrues the relationship between man and God and because signs fail where faith is absent. Benedict closes by noting that God's definitive sign for man is the Son of Man, Jesus himself.

Outline

I. The nature and purpose of the parable

  A. At the center of the teaching of Jesus

  B. Jesus' parables transcend efforts to sum them up in one literary or theological category

C. Parables describe the Kingdom of God (which comes in Jesus' Person)

D. Exposition of the parable of the sower as depicting *how* the Kingdom comes: through Jesus' apparent failure on the Cross

E. Parables require transformation on the part of the hearer and therefore convey a knowledge about God that cannot be understood if understood simply as abstract knowledge

II. Three major parables from the Gospel of Luke

A. The good Samaritan (Lk 10:25–37)

1. The Samaritan is a stranger, but it is he (not the insiders) who acts the part of the neighbor to the suffering insider

2. It requires courage to love one's neighbor

3. The Fathers find in the parable's sufferer an image of Adam, that is, of humanity alienated from God—allegorically, the stranger (unrecognized as God) binds the wounds of humanity: we are all in need of God's love so that we can love our neighbor

B. The parable of the two brothers (the prodigal son and the son who remained at home) and the good father (Lk 15:11–32)

1. One son journeys away from the father (who stands for God), and in his false autonomy ends up enslaved to sin and undergoes a conversion; in response the father forgives him and prepares a feast for him—Jesus thus explains why he welcomes and feasts with sinners

2. The other son responds bitterly, thus showing that he did not understand that by his obedience he has been enjoying true freedom rather than simply undertaking a dutiful service to his father

3. The Fathers of the Church understood the parable as God the Father's effort to persuade Israel not to be jealous of the Gentiles; Benedict accepts this interpretation so long as one notes that all the righteous, all believers, are in the position of Israel and must beware of falling into seeing worship solely as a duty to be borne

C. The parable of the rich man and Lazarus (Lk 16:19–31)

1. Lazarus embodies the cry of the poor, found in the Psalms; he also points forward to Jesus on the Cross

2. True happiness consists not in material things but in knowing God

3. The rich man is in a temporary state between death and resurrection—he asks that a sign of warning be sent to his relations

4. God's sign for man is the risen Lord, a sign that requires believing the word of Scripture

Questions for Understanding

1. What is the distinction that some scholars make between an allegory and a parable? Some scholars also insist that each parable makes "a single 'salient point' " (pp. 184–85). What limitations to these two ideas does Benedict discuss (pp. 185–86)?

2. How can the parable of the good Samaritan be understood allegorically? What is the interpretation given by the Church Fathers? By the medieval interpreters? How can one find an image of the sacraments in this parable?

3. In his discussion of Luke 15:11–32, Benedict presents different possible names for the parable most commonly referred to as the parable of the prodigal son. Why are there so many possible titles for this parable? What title does Benedict pick (pp. 202–3)? Why?

4. What are some episodes in the Old Testament where the motif of two brothers can be found (pp. 202–3)? What is another instance of this theme in the New Testament?

5. How do the Church Fathers interpret the parable of the prodigal son as an image of "Adam" (pp. 205–6)?

6. How can the parable of the prodigal son be interpreted as referring to Christ? What does it mean to see Christ as the "arm of the Father" in this parable?

7. What does Benedict designate as the "kernel" or heart of the parable of the prodigal son? What Old Testament text does he refer to in speaking of the "compassion" of the father in the parable (pp. 206–7)?

8. How does Benedict relate the parable of the rich man and Lazarus to the Psalms?

9. How does Benedict connect the parable of the rich man and Lazarus with the people seeking a sign? How is Jesus the true sign? The true Lazarus?

Questions for Application

1. While the parables of Jesus have a certain simplicity to them, Benedict reminds us that we need to turn to Jesus to understand what he is trying to teach us. Do we remember to turn to Jesus as we read the Scriptures?

2. What does Jesus say in the parable of the good Samaritan about our need to become "the neighbor"? What kind of charity does the parable prompt us to live?

3. In his interpretation of the parable of the prodigal son, Benedict points out that the arm of the father can be seen as a figure of Christ. How can this image help you to better understand the love of Jesus?

4. In the discussion of the parable of the rich man and Lazarus, Benedict refers to the distinction between true and lasting happiness and the passing pleasures of this world. How does recognizing what true happiness is give us hope?

Terms

Adolf Jülicher, 184
allegory, 184
C. W. F. Smith, 186
C. H. Dodd, 187
Levite, 196
Helmut Kuhn, 198

agape, 198
Scholastics, 200
Pierre Grelot, 202
dialectic, 203
Saint Irenaeus of Lyon, 207
Gehenna, 215

Notes

CHAPTER EIGHT

The Principal Images of John's Gospel

Summary

From discussing the parables of Jesus, found in the Synoptic Gospels (Matthew, Mark, and Luke), Benedict moves to consider John's Gospel. He examines the historicity of John's Gospel, focusing on the arguments of modern Scripture scholarship, and then he considers several key images/symbols in John—water, vine/wine, bread, and shepherd. He also shows how John's Gospel should be understood in terms of Jewish liturgy and feasts, and how Christ is revealed as the New Moses.

Benedict starts by contradicting the thesis of Rudolf Bultmann that the sources of John's Gospel are Gnostic rather than Jewish. He then takes up the question of the authorship of the Gospel and the relationship between the Gospel itself and the events it narrates. All three questions center on one fundamental question: Is the Gospel of John a reliable source for getting to know Jesus? Benedict's answer: yes. He shows how grounded the Gospel is in Jewish piety and liturgy, and he makes a historical argument that Gnosticism as a movement came onto the scene too late for the author of John to draw from it as a source.

Next, Benedict shows the plausibility of assigning authorship either to the Apostle John himself or to a close group of his associates and disciples, perhaps including a figure called Presbyter John (or John the Elder), who may have acted as a kind of literary executor for the Apostle John's work and teachings. Finally, Benedict argues that John's Gospel is not a tape recording of the events of Jesus' life, which would be an impoverished account in any case, but instead is an account that has been deepened by the author's reflection on Jesus' life and works over time and born from his deep communion with Jesus in the Holy Spirit. In this way, John's Gospel is a reliable witness to Jesus Christ, to the real Jesus.

Benedict then explores the principal images of the Gospel of John. He begins with water. In John, water primarily points to baptism, in which the Christian is reborn. The new water in which man is reborn is given by the New Moses, who surpasses the "old Moses", who also gave the people water to drink (Num 20:1–13). Jesus reveals himself as the life-giving rock from which living water flows, giving not just mere life but "life in abundance" (Jn 10:10). The way to "drink" this "water" is through faith in Jesus Christ. That water flows from Christ also marks him as the new Temple, for water flows from the side of the Jerusalem Temple in the vision of the Old Testament prophet Ezekiel (47:1–12).

Bread is a basic staple for rich and poor alike; wine represents feasting. The focus on the vine/wine image that Jesus uses in John's Gospel brings out the glory of creation. At the wedding at Cana, Jesus transforms water used for ritual purification into wine for feasting. This indicates how Jesus' coming fulfills the hope toward which purification pointed: with the coming of Jesus, the feast between God and men has begun. At the same time, the miracle at Cana looks forward toward the Cross; the superabundant flow of wine prefigures the superabundant flow of Christ's blood and also points to the Eucharistic feast of the Church.

The vine is also an image of the Church, which accomplishes the same theological purpose as the body of Christ accomplishes in Saint Paul's writings. God himself has become the vine, onto which men are grafted. Now that God has become the vine, there is no risk that he will reject or repudiate it. The fruit of the vine must be pressed into wine, and Benedict points out that the fruit of Christ, his love, is produced when he is "pressed" on the Cross. His sacrifice and purification comes before and along with his love and the salvation it accomplishes.

Both Moses and Christ give bread—God gave the manna from heaven through Moses (Ex 16:4–16). Benedict says that the bread image in John functions by contrasting Jesus' bread and Moses' bread. The manna that Moses gave only satisfies earthly hunger, but the bread Christ gives satisfies all of man's desires. Even the Torah, which is bread from heaven because it is the Word of God, Benedict points out, can only show Israel God's "back" (Ex 33:18–22) and not his "face". Jesus himself becomes our bread, which allows us to feed on God himself. This bread cannot be earned but must be received as a gift from God. The Word of God first becomes bread by becoming flesh, but ultimately becomes true bread for us in Jesus' sacrifice on the Cross and thereafter in the Eucharist.

The shepherd image in John refers to Jesus' kingship, since he is shepherd of his people. This shepherd becomes a lamb and is slain for the sheep. This establishes the pattern for all other true shepherds who come after Jesus: they must enter by the "door" of Jesus; they must imitate Jesus. Otherwise, they can only be robbers who want to exploit the sheep.

This background, Benedict says, is behind Jesus' call to Peter to "feed my sheep" (Jn 21:15–17). Peter must follow Jesus in order to be a faithful shepherd and in this way it will always be Jesus who is truly the shepherd of his people.

In laying down his life for his sheep, Jesus gives life, for he is life. Benedict points to four shepherd motifs in John. (1) Jesus is not only shepherd, but *food for the sheep*. (2) Jesus *lays down his life* for the sheep that they may have life. (3) The shepherd and the flock *know each other, by being in communion* with each other. The shepherd knows his sheep because they belong to him—not in the sense of possessions, but in the sense of responsibility—while the sheep know the shepherd because they know that they are his. (4) Jesus the shepherd *brings unity*, not only to the divided house of Israel, but to the whole world.

Outline

I. Introduction: the Johannine question

A. The Gospel of John's historical value: Rudolph Bultmann versus Martin Hengel (Pope Benedict observes that the latter biblical scholar better understands the Gospel's firsthand knowledge of Palestine in Jesus' time)

B. Who is the author of the Gospel? Pope Benedict argues that the Gospel goes back to John the son of Zebedee, the disciple of Jesus—perhaps via the "Presbyter John" described by Papias in the early third century

C. What it means for a theological text to be "historical"—needs not be verbatim, but needs to record accurately the substance of Jesus' message

D. Historical reality, recollection/memory, Church tradition, and the guidance of the Holy Spirit are all connected in the communal remembering of the Lord, in part because the Resurrection enables the disciples to understand what previously they had not understood

E. This understanding of communal remembering helps us understand the doctrine of the "inspiration" of Scripture

F. The Gospel's foundation in the Old Testament
  1. For the Gospel of John, as for the other Gospels, Jesus is the fulfillment of the prophecy in Deuteronomy 34:10, which foretells the coming of a prophet like Moses (but greater)
  2. The Gospel of John's rootedness in Israel's liturgical year (feasts)

II. The principal Johannine images

A. Water
  1. Water symbolizes rebirth (not biological life, but spiritual life); water allows for new sight; water purifies
  2. Jesus gives the living water (Jesus' body is the real Temple and the true life-giving rock)

B. Vine and wine
  1. Wine and the wedding at Cana: the marriage feast of the Lord Jesus with his bride, the Church

2. The vine and the branches (Israel as a vineyard according to Isaiah and to Jesus' parables): Jesus is the true vine, the embodiment of Israel due to the Incarnation—through purification and faith we can be his branches and bear (Eucharistic) fruit in self-giving love

C. Bread

1. Jesus' feeding miracles (e.g., multiplication of the loaves)

2. The Torah as "bread" that feeds Israel: Jesus as the living Law (the Word) who gives himself to us in the Eucharist and transforms us so long as we receive him in faith

D. The Shepherd

1. Psalm 23: God is the shepherd of Israel (see also Ezek 34–37)

2. Jesus fulfills the prophecy in Zechariah regarding the slain shepherd

3. Jesus proclaims himself to be the Good Shepherd, who suffers for the life of the sheep rather than using the sheep for his own purposes

4. Peter as the shepherd of Jesus' sheep; Peter must guide the sheep to hear Jesus' voice—Peter, like other shepherds who serve Jesus, leads the sheep not toward himself but toward God, where they find their true freedom and identity as persons

5. The sheep belong to Jesus by faith; in Jesus the sheep know the Father through the Holy Spirit and thereby enter into the Trinitarian communion

6. Jesus, the Creator (cf. Jn 1:1–3) and Redeemer, is the sole Shepherd of all men, not only of Israel—he carries us to our true home

Questions for Understanding

1. How does Benedict distinguish the Gospel of John from the Synoptics (pp. 218–19)?

2. Why would some modern biblical scholars question the "historicity" of John's Gospel (p. 219)? How does Benedict defend the historical value of John's Gospel? How does his discussion of "remembering" work to defend the "historicity" of John's Gospel?

3. How does John's Gospel serve to speak of Christ as the New Moses?

4. How does Benedict show that John's Gospel is rooted in the Old Testament and the Jewish liturgical calendar? How does this fact argue against a position that John's Gospel is a Gnostic Gospel?

5. What are the different occasions in which the symbol of water is used in John's Gospel (pp. 239–43)? How does Benedict connect Christ's promise of living water in John's Gospel with the Old Testament?

6. What are the two symbolic time references in relation to the wedding at Cana? What is the significance of Christ's "hour"?

7. In developing the symbol of bread, Benedict draws out parallels between Christ and Moses, showing that Christ surpasses Moses. What are some of these parallels? How is the manna of Moses different from the bread Christ gives?

8. How was the image of the shepherd used in the ancient Near East? How does this understanding illuminate the use of the figure of the shepherd to speak of Christ?

9. In speaking of the image of the shepherd, Benedict relates that Christ is not only identified as the shepherd, but also as the sheep gate, the sheep, and the pasture. What is the scriptural basis for identifying Christ with these different images? What do they mean when referred to Christ?

Questions for Application

1. In his discussion of "remembering", Benedict points out the role of the community in remembering as well as the role of the Holy Spirit. What role does the Church play in the "remembering" of Scripture?

2. After speaking of the prominence of liturgy in John's Gospel, Benedict makes the point that the discourses in John's Gospel are to lead us to worship (p. 238). How can such an understanding of this purpose of the discourses aid one's reading of John's Gospel?

3. Benedict's treatment of the vine provides us with a beautiful image of the spiritual life—purification that leads to bearing fruit in love, and a "remaining", which entails prayer. Are there things that we need "pruned" in our lives in order to bear "fruit" with Jesus, the true vine?

4. On page 285, Benedict provides us with a few verses from Clement of Alexandria. How can these verses be used as a prayer asking Jesus to guide us as a shepherd, to guide us to heaven?

Terms

Martin Hengel, 220

Johannine question, 222

Ulrich Wilckens, 223

Scriptura sola (sola Scriptura), 223

pied-à-terre, 225

Eusebius of Caesarea, 225

Saint Papias of Hierapolis, 225

Presbyter John, 225

E. Ruckstuhl, 226

P. Dschulnigg, 226

"Jesus poem", 228

"pneumatic Gospel", 235

Feast of Weeks (Pentecost), 237

Feast of Tabernacles, 237

Feast of the Dedication of the
    Temple (Hanukkah), 237

Photina Rech, 240

Tertullian, 240

Pool of Siloam, 242

Saint Justin, 245

Saint Hippolytus, 245

Saint Ephraim of Syria, 245

Asia Minor interpretation, 246

Alexandrian reading, 246

Gospel of Thomas, 248

Dionysus, 253

Philo of Alexandria, 253

demythologizing, 253

Logos theology, 253

Melchisedek, 253

Cardinal Christoph Schönborn, 271

C. S. Lewis, 271

Didache, 272

Hadad-Rimmon, 274

Trinitarian dialogue, 282

Roman Canon, 285

Saint Clement of Alexandria, 285

Notes

Two Milestones on Jesus' Way:
Peter's Confession and the Transfiguration

Summary

Benedict discusses in chapter eight certain key images from John's Gospel, which help us to know who Jesus is. Now, in chapter nine, Benedict explores Jesus' identity through examining Peter's confession of faith in Jesus and the revelation at the Transfiguration recounted in the Synoptic Gospels.

In each of the Synoptic Gospels, Jesus poses the question of who "the people", those outside Jesus' inner circle of friends and disciples, say that he is. He also asks who the apostles say that he is. This is the situation in which Peter's confession, his testimony about who Christ is, occurs. Benedict's account of the Transfiguration provides a deeper understanding of this event by placing it in the context of the Jewish liturgical calendar. These two events—Peter's confession and the Transfiguration—take place "on the way" to the Cross, which is the key event revealing Jesus' identity and the moment of his unveiled glory.

Peter's confession can only be understood in light of Jesus' prophesied Passion and the message of the Father after the Transfiguration in which he identifies Jesus as his Son and commands us to listen to him. Before Peter's confession, Jesus asks the disciples who "the people" say that he is. The answers all point to a similar understanding of Jesus: he is a prophet. Benedict observes that these people, who do not know Jesus as the apostles do, have something in common with some recent scholars of world religions: they recognize that there is something special about Jesus, but they do not acknowledge his uniqueness.

Jesus, contends Benedict, cannot be classified alongside other great men. Putting him next to figures such as the Buddha, Confucius, and Socrates relativizes Jesus. It makes him one among the many men whose experience one must consider in order to discover the full truth. Such an understanding makes the individual the ultimate standard of judgment and precludes genuine commitment to Jesus and his message, which is not a claim to be one among many prophets of God.

Peter declares Jesus to be the Messiah and the Son of God. Peter's confession is testimony that Jesus is unique, is different from one of the prophets. Significantly, Peter's confession happens on the Day of Atonement, when the high priest enters the Holy of Holies in the Temple and pronounces the name of God, Yahweh (YHWH). Gradually, with effort, and never perfectly or adequately until after the Resurrection, the apostles come to realize that Jesus is God.

Benedict points out that each Gospel uses slightly different wording for Peter's confession (Mk 8:29; Lk 9:20; Mt 16:16; Jn 6:69). This has led to speculation among Scripture scholars as to whether there is a development in the early Church's understanding of Jesus that is represented by these different words. Pope Benedict suspects this may be the case, but sees that each evangelist's version harmonizes with the others.

In both the confession of Peter and the Transfiguration, Jesus' divinity is front and center. In both cases, Jesus' glory is connected with his Passion. Saint Luke explicitly tells us that the topic of conversation among Moses, Elijah, and Jesus following the Transfiguration is "his exodus, which he was to accomplish at Jerusalem" (Lk 9:31). This reveals that the Passion will also be filled with God's glory.

The Transfiguration happens during the Feast of Tabernacles, in which the Jews built temporary dwellings to recall their impermanent dwellings during their forty years in the desert after the Exodus from Egypt. This feast was loaded with messianic significance in the Judaism of Jesus' time, which explains Peter's ecstasy in realizing that Jesus is fulfilling the Feast of Tabernacles before his eyes. He later needs to be reminded that the messianic age includes the Passion and Cross.

The Transfiguration takes place on a mountain, which is a counter-image of Jesus' agony in the garden, which also happens on a mountain. Jesus meets with Moses and Elijah, who symbolize the Law and the prophets of the Old Testament, and who both received revelations from God on mountains. Jesus, with whom they now speak, is God's revelation in person. This is also a reminder and a dramatic image of the reality that the Law and prophets speak of Jesus. At the end of the event, God the Father identifies Jesus as his Son and says, "Listen to him". In the context of the revelation on the mountain, which recalls the revelation of the Law to Moses on Sinai, the Father's statement means that Jesus is himself the living Torah.

Outline

I. Peter's confession

A. Peter's confession in its Gospel context

1. In the Gospels of Matthew, Mark, and Luke, Peter responds to Jesus' question "[W]ho do you say that I am?" by responding that Jesus is "the Christ, the Son of the living God" (Mt 16:15–16)

2. Jesus then tells the disciples that he will be crucified and rise again on the third day, and he instructs the disciples that they will have to "lose"

their lives in order to "find" them: Peter's confession of Jesus is linked to the radically self-giving way of life that the disciples must follow

3. In the Synoptic Gospels, the event following Peter's confession is Jesus' Transfiguration, where Jesus' status as the Son is attested to by the Father, Moses (the Law), and Elijah (the prophets)

4. John 6:68–69 also describes Peter's confession of Jesus' messianic lordship ("the Holy One of God"), and he connects this confession with the Eucharist and with the Eucharistic way of life that the disciples will have to follow

B. At Caesarea Philippi, Jesus is starting his ascent to Jerusalem

1. Jesus at prayer with his Father, with the disciples with him (Gospel of Luke)

2. The deeper knowledge of Jesus that the disciples possess, enabling them to identify him in his newness and uniqueness (others think of Jesus simply as a prophet, even though they see him as a prophet who may accomplish the restoration of Israel and the New Covenant)

3. Jesus is not merely a "great religious founder" who has a powerful human experience of God

4. Jesus seeks to clarify the meaning of "Messiah"—not earthly power, but the Cross (and Resurrection)—the Son of God who empties himself in humility (cf. Phil 2)

5. A meaning of "Messiah" that the mere perspective of "flesh and blood" cannot understand, as is shown when Jesus' accusers ask him whether he is the "Anointed One" and when they mock him on the Cross as the "Chosen One"

C. Distinction between the commission given to Peter and the one later given to Paul

D. Parallels to Peter's confession at Caesarea Philippi

1. The miraculous catch of fish that leads Peter and his companions to become disciples (Gospel of Luke)—Peter recognizes God working through Jesus, and proclaims Jesus' lordship and his own sinfulness

2. Jesus' walking on water that leads Peter, and the other disciples, to proclaim him to be the Son of God, because God's power is working through Jesus

3. Peter's confession of faith after Jesus' Eucharistic discourse in John 6 shows the relationship of Peter's confession (of God's power in Jesus) to the Cross—not earthly power but power through self-giving, sacrificial love

E. The scandal of Jesus

    1. He does *not* seek earthly power in the way that false messiahs, such as Barabbas, do—thus he is recognized as the Messiah with greater difficulty

    2. He suggests that he is equal to God: his newness and uniqueness, beyond any prophet

F. The Church's mission is to proclaim and enter into this mystery ever more deeply

II. The Transfiguration

A. The Jewish festivals and the relationship of Jesus' glory to his Cross

    1. Van Cangh and van Esbroeck's argument that Peter's confession of Jesus as Messiah and Son of God occurred on the Jewish festival of the Day of Atonement, while Jesus' Transfiguration took place on the last day of the Feast of Tabernacles

    2. Gese's argument that Exodus 24—Moses' sealing (by sacrificial blood) of the covenant of Israel with the Lord, his ascent of Mount Sinai with the elders, and their eating and drinking in the presence of the Lord—forms the background to Jesus' Transfiguration

B. The Transfiguration narrative and the relationship of Jesus' glory to his Cross

    1. Jesus takes Peter, James, and John, as he does also for his agony in the Garden of Gethsemane

    2. The mountain is a symbol of God's closeness; mountains can be found at every crucial step of Jesus' life, as well as in the history of Israel (including Moses' and Elijah's encounter with God)

    3. Jesus goes up the mountain to pray (Gospel of Luke), and his face and clothes are transfigured before his disciples, due to the intensity and perfection of his communion with the Father—Jesus' true divine being is revealed

    4. Jesus' transfigured face and clothes point, as well, to the glorification of the saints (compare with the Book of Revelation), who have been purified and united with Jesus

    5. Jesus' speaking with Moses and Elijah makes clear that the Law and the prophets speak of (and thus with) Jesus: they speak about his Cross, his new Exodus by which he leads man from slavery to sin into eternal life with God

6. Jesus' Cross is no mere suffering; it is filled with divine glory and power

7. Jesus teaches Peter, James, and John that Elijah, in John the Baptist, has already returned and suffered a fate (beheading) that prepares for the Messiah's Cross

C. Jean Daniélou on the connection between the Feast of Tabernacles and the Transfiguration

1. The Feast of Tabernacles looks forward to the restoration of Israel, in which the just would dwell with God

2. Connection of the Feast of Tabernacles with John 1:14, the Word's "tabernacling" in the Incarnation (Saint Gregory of Nyssa)

3. The true Feast of Tabernacles has arrived

D. The Father's voice out of the cloud: the Father proclaims Jesus' Sonship; the cloud of God's presence will overshadow all who listen to Jesus (Jesus as the new Torah)

E. The Transfiguration reveals the beginning of the messianic age, the Kingdom of God that Jesus' Cross and Resurrection inaugurate

Questions for Understanding

1. What is the connection Benedict draws between Peter's confession and the Transfiguration?

2. Why do the disciples recognize who Jesus is when "the people" do not? What is the root of the disciples' understanding (p. 291)?

3. Like Karl Jaspers, many today put Jesus in a class together with Socrates, Buddha, and Confucius (p. 292). How is this like the opinion of "the people" that Jesus is a prophet from the past?

4. How is the commission given to Peter fundamentally different from the commission given to Paul (p. 297)?

5. Why does Pope Benedict say that scholarship "overplays its hand" by trying to reconstruct the original words of Peter's confession and attribute everything else to later developments (p. 303)?

6. How is Peter's confession more accurate than the opinion of "the people" (p. 304)? How is his confession still limited and open to further understanding?

7. Why is it that we only recognize Jesus correctly when we put together his divinity and the Cross (p. 305)? One might think that divinity and suffering are

contraries. How does Jesus' suffering on the Cross in fact reveal something about his divinity?

8. What three dimensions does every Jewish feast contain (p. 307)?

9. Moses shone with light after speaking with God on Mount Sinai, and Jesus shone with light on the Mount of Transfiguration. What is the difference between the light of Moses and the light of Jesus (p. 310)?

10. How does the conversation between Jesus and Moses and Elijah, as recorded in Luke's Gospel, connect the ideas of glorification and suffering (p. 311)?

11. If we understand the Transfiguration against the background of Exodus 24 and 33, what does Peter intend to accomplish by erecting three booths (p. 313)?

12. If we understand the Transfiguration against the background of the Feast of Tabernacles, what does Peter mean by suggesting that they build three booths (p. 315)?

13. How does the scene of the Transfiguration show that Jesus himself is the Torah (p. 316)?

Questions for Application

1. Benedict connects deeper knowledge to discipleship. How do we come to know Jesus more intimately through following him?

2. What is the link between Jesus' Cross and his glory? How does this affect your life?

3. Through prayer, we are invited to go with Christ to the mountain. How can we find in the Transfiguration an image of what happens when we encounter Christ in prayer?

4. Like Peter, we may take the Lord aside in order to say to him: "God forbid it, Lord! This shall never happen to you!" And because we doubt that God really will forbid the way of the Cross, we may ourselves try to prevent it (p. 299). What would change in our daily lives if we fully accepted the way of the Cross in our lives?

5. Confronted with the presence of God in Jesus, Peter is shaken to the core of his being. He realizes how pitifully small he is, and he cannot bear the awe-inspiring grandeur of God—it is too enormous for him (p. 301). When we come into the

presence of Jesus at Mass, do we realize how awe-inspiring that Real Presence is? Or do we comfort ourselves by thinking of Jesus only as a friendly, saintly man?

6. The union of hope for salvation and the Passion of the Christ fits with Scripture's deepest message, but seeing these two seemingly contradictory things as God's plan was still a startling novelty in Jesus' day (pp. 312–13). What can we do to learn from Jesus how to read Scripture afresh and be startled?

Terms

sanctuary of Pan, 289
Herod the Great, 289
Karl Jaspers, 292
Socrates, 292
Buddha, 292
Confucius, 292
Communio/koinonia, 296

Kyrios, 301
Yom ha-Kippurim, 306
Sukkoth, 306
Jean Daniélou, 306
H. Gese, 307
Harald Riesenfeld, 314
Saint Gregory of Nyssa, 315

Notes

CHAPTER TEN

Jesus Declares His Identity

Summary

Having considered how others speak of Jesus, Benedict turns to how *Jesus* speaks of himself. "Son of Man" and "Son" are two "titles" that Jesus applies to himself in the Gospels. Benedict also treats the "I am" sayings of Jesus, showing that these are found in the Synoptic Gospels as well as in the Gospel of John.

That Jesus is "the Son" has never been disputed in the Church; what this teaching means, on the other hand, has been a source of controversy from the beginning. Benedict points out that the only Greek philosophical term used in the Nicene Creed, *homooúsios*, is used to clarify the meaning of Jesus' Sonship: he is *homooúsios*, "one in being" with the Father. Far from imposing foreign categories, this term preserves and protects the biblical testimony from distortions, especially by those who would read Jesus' being the Son of God as a political or mythological title rather than a matter of his very being.

Many contemporary Scripture scholars deny that most of the "Son of Man" sayings in the Gospels come from Jesus. They think that these sayings were put on the lips of Jesus by his later followers. Advocates of this view, Benedict says, think Jesus preached an imminent end of the world and that the Son of Man was someone else associated with the end, not Jesus himself.

Benedict rejects this idea as unsupported by the evidence. He argues that Jesus must have spoken about himself when using provocative terms such as the Son of Man. Otherwise, we cannot account for the extraordinary measures the Jewish leaders took to execute Jesus or the massive effect Jesus had on his followers. The earliest interpreters of Jesus took him as referring to himself when he spoke of the Son of Man. All of the Son of Man sayings in the Gospels can reasonably be read this way. The best explanation, then, is that Jesus claimed something extraordinary and astonishing: that he was the Son of Man.

The title of "son of man" is used in the book of Daniel (7:13). He is a heavenly figure who represents the universal Kingdom of God, as opposed to the various earthly kingdoms represented in Daniel by a number of grotesque beasts. Benedict holds that

Jesus took up the term "Son of Man" and applied it to himself. He was able to give this term the meaning he wanted in order to refer to his ministry.

The title "Son of Man" is fundamentally about Jesus' role as mediator and judge. Jesus is fully man because he comes from God and returns to God, providing a model for all men. He judges men as a man himself. Becoming man, he has put himself in solidarity with all the victims of sin and injustice in history, having himself suffered monumental injustice and sin as a man. Jesus' Cross and his glory are inherently united and inseparable. The Son of Man is perfect man, Benedict observes, but he is also the one who undergoes the pain and suffering of the Passion. It is precisely the divine claim of the Son of Man that leads to the Passion; nothing else can account for it. This reveals what God's lordship really means: love, service, self-emptying, and humility.

As the Son of Man, Christ renews humanity; discipleship in Christ entails a renewal in man. As mediator, the Son of Man brings God to man and man to God through his solidarity with men in his life and his suffering death; as a fellow man who has suffered the gravest injustice, the Son of Man is a judge who fully knows man's plight.

The title "son of God" originates in ancient Near Eastern political theology, in which the king of the people is referred to as "son of God". Israel's king was also identified as the son of God: his coronation ritual included words of divine adoption. Israel itself is referred to as God's son (see Ex 4:22). Israel's sonship is personified in the king. Benedict argues that the promise that Israel will rule all nations clearly points beyond the present king and the present kingdom, which never even approached world dominion. This promise always remains Israel's hope, until the coming of Christ, whose kingdom is not built by earthly power, but by love and faith, and who does not rule from a standard throne, but from the throne of the Cross. The Church therefore always stands against totalitarianism, following her Master in martyrdom when confronted with the absolute claims of earthly powers.

Only the Son knows the Father; but knowing always implies a kind of equality. The Son's claim to know the Father, then, is a claim of equality with the Father; it is a claim to *be* God. Christ's communion with the Father is in knowledge and also in will. He is utterly obedient to the Father, providing a way for men to follow him in his obedience. Only the Son reveals the Father since only the Son knows the Father. But he does not reveal haphazardly; he reveals to the pure of heart, to the simple, the ones who are obedient to the Father and do not regard themselves as self-sufficient. Jesus' relationship with the Father in knowledge and will reveals his uniqueness: although the prophets and Moses prefigure him, there is no one who can claim to pray to the Father as "Abba", on terms so intimate. Not even Moses and the prophets call Yahweh (YHWH) "Abba".

The "I am" statements reveal Jesus' divinity by alluding to Yahweh's name, which means "I am". There are two kinds of these statements by Jesus: simple "I am" statements and those that further specify him, such as "the Bread of Life" and "the light of the world". The simple "I am" statements are like the revelation from the burning bush (Ex 3:14), in which God reveals his name as "I am who I am" (Yahweh, YHWH). By this he shows that he is the One who simply *is* without qualification. This is both to distinguish Yahweh from other, pagan gods and to reveal positively God's absolute oneness.

When Jesus says "I am" or "I am he", he identifies himself with the Father; it is when Jesus is exalted on the Cross that this oneness with the Father is fully visible. The revelation from the burning bush and the revelation on the Cross are one. The "I am" statements all refer to one thing: man wants one thing, happiness, and only Jesus brings happiness because Jesus brings God. Jesus brings God because Jesus is God. He is "consubstantial", *homooúsios*, "one in being", with the Father.

Outline

I. Introduction: titles of Jesus

A. Christ/Messiah, Kyrios (Lord), Son of God

B. "Christ" soon became used as his name ("Jesus Christ") because his mission and his Person are one

C. Kyrios and Son of God connote his communion with the divine Father, his divinity and Sonship

D. Jesus' preferred titles for himself are "Son of Man" and the "Son"—Pope Benedict wishes to focus on these two titles

II. The Son of Man

A. Saint Stephen's words at his martyrdom: "I see the heavens opened, and the Son of man standing at the right hand of God" (Acts 7:56)—this vision is what Jesus promised at his trial, in Mark 14:62

B. Three sets of Son of Man sayings, regarding which contemporary biblical exegetes often accept only the first set (if that) as coming from Jesus himself

1. Sayings that describe the Son of Man who is to come and that seem to distinguish the Son of Man from Jesus—Pope Benedict goes on to show that the Son of Man is identical with Jesus

2. Sayings about the earthly work of the Son of Man

3. Sayings about the Son of Man's Cross and Resurrection

C. By contrast to exegetes who minimize the latter two sets of sayings, Pope Benedict points out that the Church would have had nothing to remember had Jesus not been dramatically new

D. How "Son of Man" fits Jesus' ministry

    1. "Son of Man" fits with Jesus' parabolic style of teaching; it also fits with his introduction of a new freedom (under his lordship) for man

    2. "Son of man" was not a title used in first-century Judaism, but it relates to the prophecy of Daniel 7

    3. Connection between Jesus' "Son of Man" saying during his trial, and his use of the "Son of Man" in his parable about the Last Judgment in Matthew 25—Pope Benedict explores the connections between Jesus' solidarity with those who suffer, and Jesus' glory as the "Son of Man"

E. The Son of Man, divine authority, and human suffering

    1. Jesus is identical with the "Son of Man", and as such he claims divine authority (e.g., Mk 2)

    2. The "son of man" is the Suffering Servant, thereby combining Daniel's image of power with Isaiah 53's image of redemptive suffering (see also the suffering of the innocent man in Wisdom 2)

    3. Jesus is the true "Son of Man" because, as the Son of God incarnate, he reveals the true form of human existence (the new Adam)—united with his new humanity, by living as he lived, we exist in communion with God

III. The Son

A. "Son of God", as a title, has origins in Egypt and Babylon, where the king was called "son of God"—it also has origins in Israel's role as YHWH's "first-born son" (Ex 4:22) and in YHWH's fatherhood to the son of David (2 Sam 7:12)—see also Psalms 2 and 89

    1. The Davidic king embodies Israel's status as YHWH's son

    2. Election (of Israel) and begetting (of God's son)

    3. Promise of a future Davidic king who will have dominion over all nations

B. The Resurrection of Jesus as the fulfillment of what was promised about Israel and the Davidic king as the "son of God"—the risen Jesus' dominion and kingship is that of spiritual communion (oneness with God) rather than worldly political power—contrast with the claims of Egypt, Babylon, and Rome

C. Only the Son knows the Father

    1. The Son is therefore equal with the Father (perfect communion in knowledge = perfect communion in being)

   2. Our knowledge of the Father is a participation in the Son's knowing

   3. The Son's will is also identical to the Father's, and in the Son we too are united in will to the Father

D. The Father and Son will to draw the simple, not the proudly wise, into union with God—those who are pure of heart are simple

E. Sonship is relational, and therefore no one who aims for autonomy can find sonship—childlike dependence is required

F. The Synoptic Gospels and the Gospel of John accord with each other as regards the Son

   1. Both present the Father as giving himself entirely to the Son, and the Son as giving himself entirely to the world in love (Cross)

   2. Both present Jesus' prayer as the heart of his filial dialogue with the Father—God is Trinitarian communion

G. We share in the Son's intimate relation with his Father, even though only Jesus is "Son"

IV. "I Am"

A. "[Y]ou will die in your sins unless you believe that I am he" (Jn 8:24)

   1. The background to this saying is Exodus 3:14, where God names himself "I AM"

   2. Isaiah 43: "I am He"

   3. Oneness of the Father and the Son

B. "When you have lifted up the Son of man, then you will know that I am he" (Jn 8:28)

   1. Connection of the "I am" (the God of the burning bush) with the Cross

   2. Pentecost inaugurates the world's knowing of Jesus as God

C. "[B]efore Abraham was, I am" (Jn 8:58)

   1. Transcends the created realm

   2. Jesus' divine mode of being

D. "[I]t is I [I am he]; have no fear!" (Mk 6:50)

   1. Fear in the presence of God's power

   2. Theophany and adoration

E. The seven "I am" statements in the Gospel of John: the bread of life; the light of the world; the door; the good shepherd; the resurrection and the life; the way, the truth, and the life; the true vine

     1. Jesus gives true life, the fullness of life, happiness (the Kingdom of God)

     2. Man needs God; Jesus gives God to us, because he is God/Life

  F. The titles of Jesus reveal how he fulfills Israel's Scriptures, and the true meaning of these titles is defended in the Nicene Creed, which we profess in the Church

Questions for Understanding

1. At the beginning of the chapter, Benedict identifies three titles that were used in the early Christian community to speak of Jesus. What are these (p. 319)? What are the two "titles" that Jesus uses in reference to himself in the Gospels (p. 321)?

2. Why might Jesus not use the title "Messiah" in referring to himself (p. 321)? Where does this term finally "appear"? Why would it be appropriate that it be used at this moment in the life of Christ (p. 321)?

3. How do the terms "Son of Man" and "Son" differ? Where did these terms come from?

4. What does the title Son of Man mean? How is "son of man" used in Daniel 7 (pp. 325–26)?

5. When Jesus says "I am he" what does this mean? What is the significance of this statement? How does this statement contain a reference to the Father? What does it say about Jesus' relation to the Father?

6. What is the connection that Benedict makes between the Cross and the burning bush of Exodus? How are these both important moments of God's revelation of himself to man?

7. What are the seven (or eight) "I am" sayings connected to a particular image in the Gospel of John (pp. 352–53)? On what theme do all of these sayings converge (p. 353)?

8. Benedict speaks of how man both needs and desires "one thing". What are the different ways that he speaks of man's desire for the "one thing" (pp. 353–54)? How does Jesus fulfill this need/desire?

9. What does Benedict see as the Church's role in helping to clarify language about Christ (pp. 354–55)?

Questions for Application

1. Jesus spoke of himself as "Son". As "sons in the Son", how should we live in awareness of our relation to the Father?

2. What is the *Jubelruf* that Benedict refers to (pp. 339–40)? What Scripture is this based on? How can our prayer at times be made as a "joyful cry", a hymn of praise to God?

3. It is not the scholar of the Law who recognizes Jesus but the simple (p. 342). How does one come to know God through being simple? How does Benedict show a correspondence between simplicity and purity of heart (p. 343)? How can you become simpler in a way that will lead you deeper in your relationship with Christ?

4. Read the last line of chapter ten (p. 355). In what way does Benedict place himself here at the end of the book? How can we join our confession with that of Peter?

Terms

homooúsios, 320   consubstantial, 355

Notes

Glossary

Adam, Karl, xi. Prolific German theologian (1876–1966). Adam was persecuted for a time because of his anti-Nazi teachings. The young Joseph Ratzinger read Adam's life of Christ when he was growing up.

agape, 198. Greek word for "love". The Greek language has several words for the English "love", all connoting different kinds of love, including *eros* (most commonly, sexual love) and *philia* (which means something like friendship or friendliness, although broader than that). *Agape*, on the other hand, is most accurately translated in its Christian usage by "charity", or divine love.

Alexandrian reading, 246. Interprets John 7:38, "Out of his heart [body] shall flow rivers of living water", as referring to the body of the Christian believer. This interpretation is championed by Origen, Jerome, and Augustine.

allegory, 184. One of the so-called four senses of Scripture. Traditionally, these four senses are divided into one literal sense and three spiritual senses: the allegorical sense, which deals with the way other biblical realities, like the Passover lamb, point to or are fulfilled or brought to light in Christ; the tropological or moral sense, which deals with the way in which Scripture exhorts right action; and the anagogical sense, which deals with the way in which Scripture points us to heaven. Christian allegory is distinguished from the allegory of the ancient Greeks in that ancient Greek allegory consciously reinterprets texts found to have an unacceptable meaning, while Christian allegory sees the realities that scriptural texts point to as having a unity and intelligibility due to divine providence that the interpreter discovers.

analogy of faith, xviii. The concept that, because of the unity of Christian teaching, each doctrine sheds light on every other doctrine and ought to be read in light of the whole Christian faith. The term is originally found in Romans 12:6.

Anthony, Saint, 77. Also known as Saint Anthony of the Desert. Early Egyptian hermit; often referred to as the father of Christian monasticism. Anthony, who lived from the middle of the third to the middle of the fourth centuries, is primarily known through the biography written by Saint Athanasius, *The Life of Anthony.*

"The Antichrist", by Vladimir Soloviev, 35. Short story depicting the rise of a modern antichrist, written by the nineteenth-century Russian philosopher.

apodictic law, 123. Type of Old Testament law that comes directly from God and one that therefore holds for all times and places, and is not subject to revision.

Apostles' Creed, 26. Ancient creed of the Church, the origin of which tradition ascribes to the apostles.

Artus, Olivier, 124. Contemporary French Catholic Old Testament scholar; member of the Pontifical Biblical Commission.

Asia Minor interpretation, 246. Interprets John 7:38, "Out of his heart [body] shall flow rivers of living water", as referring to Christ's body. This interpretation is championed by Justin Martyr, Irenaeus of Lyon, Hippolytus of Rome, Cyprian, and Ephraim of Syria, as well as the modern Catholic biblical scholar Rudolf Schnackenburg.

Augustine, Saint, 24. Bishop, theologian, and Doctor of the Church who lived from A.D. 354 to 430 and is sometimes called the "Second Founder of the Faith" (Saint Jerome) because of his gigantic literary, theological, and pastoral contribution to Christianity.

Augustus, 11. Great Roman emperor from 27 B.C. to A.D. 14 who styled himself the savior of mankind and the bringer of peace. The universalistic claims of Augustus, along with other Roman emperors, are often the unspoken backdrop to Jesus' teaching in the Gospels.

autobasileia, 49. Greek word describing Christ's personification of the Kingdom of God.

Bar-Kokhba, 41. Simon Bar-Kokhba (meaning "son of the star" in Hebrew); led a revolt against Roman occupation of Judea in A.D. 132. He succeeded in his initial attempt and ruled Judea for three years as an independent country, after which the Romans committed twelve legions of troops to take Judea back and Bar-Kokhba was defeated. He consciously presented himself as a messianic figure.

Barabbas, 40. Political revolutionary whose agitations were put down by the Romans. The crowds asked Pontius Pilate to release from custody Barabbas, a political messianic figure, instead of Jesus (Mt 27:15–21; Mk 15:6–11; Lk 23:13–18; Jn 18:39–40).

Benedict, Saint, 131. Italian saint and founder of the Order of Saint Benedict; he is often called the father of Western monasticism. He was born in Nursia around A.D. 480 and died at his abbey, Monte Cassino, around A.D. 547.

Bernard of Clairvaux, Saint, 87. Cistercian abbot, theologian, and Doctor of the Church (1090–1153).

Bloch, Ernst, 53. German Marxist philosopher (1885–1977).

Book of the Covenant, 123. Section of the Book of Exodus that lays out the Law of Moses in a concise way.

Buber, Martin, 144. German Jewish philosopher, Scripture scholar, and political activist (1878–1965). Buber was influenced by existentialism. His writing emphasized the presence of God, but de-emphasized Jewish Law. His most famous work is perhaps *I-Thou*.

Buddha, 292. Fifth century B.C. Indian ascetic and spiritual teacher; regarded as the founder of Buddhism.

Bultmann, Rudolf, 48. German Protestant biblical scholar and theologian (1884–1976) who attempted to "de-mythologize" Christianity—to separate what he considered the essence of Christianity from the worldview of the scriptural authors, which he regarded as mythological. Bultmann was also among the leading proponents of "form criticism". He also maintained that the Gospels were not historical narratives but theology reshaped into the form of a story. He believed that Christianity needed to be understood in terms of the early philosophy of Martin Heidegger rather than what he regarded as the mythical worldview of the biblical writers.

canonical exegesis, xviii. An approach to interpreting parts of the Bible by trying to understand them as part of the whole "canon" of the Bible. This approach is often associated with the Protestant biblical scholar and theologian Brevard Childs (1920–2007), although it is not distinctly Protestant.

casuistic law, 123. Type of Old Testament law that is not directly from God and which is historically conditioned and open to revision; it is formulated according to the needs of the time and based upon divine law.

Christocentrism, 53. Theological view that Christ is the center of Christianity, as opposed to God (theocentrism), the Church (ecclesiocentrism) or the Kingdom of God (regnocentrism).

Clement of Alexandria, Saint, 285. Father of the Church and the head of the catechetical school in Alexandria in the latter part of the second century.

communio/koinonia, 296. *Communio* is the Latin and *koinonia* the Greek word for "communion" or "fellowship".

Confucius, 292. Chinese philosopher, political theorist, and ethicist who lived in the fifth century B.C.

consubstantial, 355. Theological term describing the kind of unity Jesus has with God the Father. The term means that the Son and the Father share the same "substance" or divine existence. They are both the one God. The term is translated "one in being" in the English version of the Nicene Creed.

Crüsemann, Frank, 125. Contemporary German Protestant Old Testament scholar; born in 1938.

Cyprian, Saint, 131. Third-century martyr and bishop of Antioch.

Cyril of Jerusalem, Saint, 19. Church Father, theologian, and Doctor of the Church (347–407). He served as bishop of Jerusalem.

Daniel-Rops, Henri, xi. French Church historian, editor, and novelist (1901–1965) whose life of Christ, *Jesus, His Life and Times,* influenced Joseph Ratzinger/Benedict XVI. Daniel-Rops was a pen name; his real name was Henry Jules Charles Petiot.

Daniélou, Jean, 306. French Catholic cardinal and theologian (1904–1974) who was one of the leaders of the *Ressourcement* movement in twentieth-century Catholic theology, which sought to return to the foundational sources of the faith in Scripture, the Fathers of the Church, and the medieval scholastics.

de Lubac, Henri, 173. French cardinal and theologian (1896–1991). De Lubac was one of the leaders of the twentieth-century *Ressourcement* movement in Catholic theology, which was an effort to retrieve the great sources of Catholic theology in Scripture, the Fathers of the Church, and the medieval scholastics. Joseph Ratzinger/Benedict XVI was greatly influenced by de Lubac, especially by his book *Catholicism.*

Delp, Alfred, 33. Anti-Nazi German Jesuit priest (1907–1945); executed by the Nazi regime in 1945.

demythologizing, 253. An approach that seeks to go beyond what an interpreter regards as mythological elements in a text in order to establish what he holds to be its real meaning. Benedict calls Philo of Alexandria's method of rationally purifying Greek myth to accord with philosophy and Jewish faith "demythologizing". In the twentieth century Rudolph Bultmann was famous for seeking to "demythologize" the New Testament, including its portrayal of Jesus.

dialectic, 203. The interaction and working out of conflicting ideas or claims; from the Greek *dialektike,* meaning "argumentative".

Didache, 272. Later first-century or early second-century Christian catechetical text, which gives instruction in doctrine, morals, the hierarchy of the Church, and the celebration of sacraments. *Didache* means "teaching" in Greek.

Dionysus, 253. Greek god of wine who was celebrated in pagan liturgical revels.

Divino Afflante Spiritu, xiv. Encyclical letter issued by Pope Pius XII in 1943 on the topic of Sacred Scripture. It permitted the limited use of the historical-critical method. Its teaching was later developed by Vatican II's *Dei Verbum (Dogmatic Constitution on Divine Revelation).*

Dodd, C. H., 187. Welsh Protestant New Testament scholar (1884–1973) who argued for "realized eschatology", the idea that the Kingdom of God is a present reality and not merely a future event. He criticized the idea that Jesus taught that the Kingdom was yet to come. Dodd taught that the Kingdom arrived in the Person of Jesus.

doxa, 39. Greek word meaning "glory" or "splendor". Benedict uses it to refer to the false splendor of earthly kingdoms, in contrast with the true splendor of the Kingdom of God.

Dschulnigg, P., 226. Scholarly collaborator of E. Ruckstuhl. See glossary entry for E. Ruckstuhl.

ecclesiocentrism, 53. Theological tendency to treat the Church as if it were the center of Christianity, as opposed to Christ (Christocentrism), God (theocentrism), or the Kingdom of God (regnocentrism).

Elliger, Karl, 81. German scripture scholar (1901–1977).

Ephraim of Syria, Saint, 245. Fourth-century Syriac theologian, Doctor of the Church, deacon, and hymnographer.

epiousios, 153. Greek word in the fourth petition of the Lord's Prayer (Mt 6:11) translated into English as "daily"; comes from *epi*, meaning "over" or "above", and *ousios*, meaning "being" or "substance".

eschatological, 4. Relating to the study of the "last things" or the final destiny of man and the world.

Essenes, 13. A Jewish ascetical sect that existed in Palestine from the second century B.C. to the First Jewish Revolt and Fall of Jerusalem, c. A.D. 65–70. The community at Qumran, with which the Dead Sea Scrolls are associated, is generally thought to have been made up of Essenes, although the sect also had members who lived in villages. The Essenes were critical of the religious establishment in Jerusalem and they regarded the worship at the Temple in Jerusalem as corrupt. They also anticipated an eschatological "showdown" between "the sons of light" (themselves) and "the sons of darkness", the enemies of God's righteous people.

Et incarnatus est, xv. A phrase of the Nicene Creed in Latin, which translated means "and was incarnated". The phrase refers to the Christian doctrine of the Incarnation, which holds that the Son of God took on a human nature and became man.

Eusebius of Caesarea, 225. Influential Church historian and bishop of Caesarea-Palestina (c. 263–c. 339); sometimes called "the father of Church history" because of his *History of the Church.*

evangelium, 47. From the Greek word *euangelion,* for "good news", it refers to a saving message. Roman emperors used this word to describe their own messages; the Gospel writers took over the term *evangelion* to refer to the saving message of the Kingdom of God preached by Jesus. The English word "gospel" is used to translate it.

Evdokimov, Paul, 19. French Eastern Orthodox theologian (1902–1970).

exegesis, xiii. The process of trying to understand what a text means.

Feast of the Dedication of the Temple (Hanukkah), 237. Feast of Lights, encompassing eight nights commemorating the dedication of the Second Temple in the second century B.C.

Feast of Tabernacles, 237. Also called the Feast of Booths, a biblical pilgrimage feast lasting seven days in which observers build temporary dwellings to recall the temporary dwellings the Israelites used in their forty-year sojourn in the desert after the Exodus (see Lev 23:33–36; Deut 16:13–15). Jesus gave his "rivers of living water" discourse (Jn 7:38) in the context of this feast (Jn 7:2, 37).

Feast of Weeks (Pentecost), 237. Jewish feast mentioned in John 5:1 commemorating the giving of the Ten Commandments to Moses. For this feast all Jewish males are required to travel to the Temple in Jerusalem. The first Pentecost after the Resurrection was the date of the descent of the Holy Spirit on the apostles (Acts 2:1–4). Jesus heals the paralytic in the context of this feast (Jn 5:1, 5–9).

Francis of Assisi, Saint, 77. Italian founder of the Order of Friars Minor, or Franciscans (1181/1182–1226); known for his radical embrace of poverty.

Francis Xavier, Saint, 162. Spanish co-founder of the Society of Jesus and missionary to India and Asia (1506–1552).

Gehenna, 215. A final place of punishment for the wicked in the New Testament (Mt 10:28; 23:33; Mk 9:43); named after a burning garbage dump, in a supposedly cursed valley near Jerusalem, where child sacrifices were made to the pagan god Moloch.

Gese, H., 307. Contemporary German Old Testament scholar.

Gnilka, Joachim, 15. Contemporary Scripture scholar writing in German; born 1928.

Gospel of Thomas, 248. A writing discovered at Nag Hammadi in Egypt in 1945 containing sayings attributed to Jesus, most of which are not found in the four Gospels of the New Testament. This document is generally regarded as having been created by Gnostic Christians in the mid-second century. Scholars are divided about how much, if any, of the material in this work goes back to Jesus. Most scholars acknowledge that the work uses a great deal of material from the Gospels of the New Testament but alters this material to reflect Gnostic ideas.

Gregory of Nyssa, Saint, 315. Bishop of Nyssa in Cappadocia (modern-day Turkey), theologian, and saint. Gregory is one of the Cappadocian Fathers along with his brother Saint Basil and Saint Gregory Nazianzen, who associated together and shared similar educational backgrounds. All three were active in the Trinitarian controversies of the fourth century.

Grelot, Pierre, 202. French Catholic priest, theologian, and former member of the Pontifical Biblical Commission (b. 1917). Grelot has written on topics of exegesis, biblical symbolism, and interreligious dialogue.

Guardini, Romano, xi. Influential Italian-German theologian (1885–1968). Guardini wrote on a wide variety of topics, including the liturgy and the historical character of Christian revelation. He wrote *The Lord,* a life of Christ inspirational to Pope Benedict in the writing of *Jesus of Nazareth.*

Hadad-Rimmon, 274. Located in the valley of Megiddo, Hadad-Rimmon was a town named after two pagan vegetation deities, Hadad and Rimmon, whose mythologies included their dying and rising; Hadad-Rimmon was the site of lamentation for the death of Israelite King Josiah, who is credited in 2 Kings 21–23 with the return of Israel to the worship of YHWH and obedience to the Law of Moses from the idolatry of his father, King Menasseh.

Heidegger, Martin, 53. German philosopher (1889–1976) who posited that being is prior to nonbeing. Heidegger greatly influenced major thinkers such as Jacques Derrida, Hans-Georg Gadamer, Leo Strauss, Jean-Paul Sartre, Hannah Arendt, and Karl Rahner, among many others. Bultmann assimilated Heidegger's philosophy in his eschatology, allowing Bultmann to try to explain Christian faith in an eschatological context of standing ready for the challenge of the Gospel.

Hengel, Martin, 220. German scholar of religion (b. 1926) focusing on Christian and Jewish religions from 200 B.C. to A.D. 200. His scholarship undermines the influential position of Rudolf Bultmann that the sources of the Gospel of John are Gnostic rather than Jewish.

Herod the Great, 289. Roman-backed ruler of Judea from 37 B.C. to 4 B.C. Herod was known for his building projects, including rebuilding of the Temple in Jerusalem.

Hippolytus, Saint, 245. A priest of Rome, a prolific theologian, and a sometime schismatic bishop who was later reconciled to the Catholic Church and died a martyr around the year 236.

historical-critical scholarship, xii. Broad term for a modern method of understanding biblical texts by drawing exclusively on the findings of the human sciences, including history, linguistics and philology, comparative literature and textual criticism, and archaeology. The method seeks primarily to know the meaning of the text when it was originally written and received. It does not presuppose the divine inspiration of the Bible.

"historical Jesus" and "Christ of faith", xi. The distinction between Jesus as he is thought to have really been and what the Church believes about him. When the distinction is used to suggest that the Jesus of history is different from what the Church believes about him, Benedict regards the distinction as the result of misusing the historical-critical method. He holds the Jesus of the Gospels, the Christ of the Church's faith, to be the "real" Jesus—Jesus as he really is. Benedict holds the Gospels' and the Church's Jesus to be a historically plausible and convincing person.

Homeric epics, 98. The *Iliad* and the *Odyssey*, both by the classical Greek poet Homer. The former tells the story of the quarrel between Achilles and Agamemnon during the siege of Troy; the latter of the return home of Odysseus from the Trojan War.

homooúsios, 320. Greek word meaning "same substance". It is used as a theological term to explain the way in which Jesus and God the Father are the same God. The term means that the Son and the Father share the same "substance" or divine being. It is a Greek term closely tied to the word "consubstantial", from the Latin word *consubstantialis.*

infancy narratives, xxiv. Sections of Matthew (1:18—2:23) and Luke (1:5—2:52) that recount the events surrounding Jesus' birth and early childhood.

Inferno, 20. Epic poem by the late thirteenth-, early fourteenth-century Italian author Dante Alighieri (1265–1321) narrating his fictional journey through hell. It is part of the work known as *The Divine Comedy.*

inspiration, xx. The theological doctrine that the Holy Spirit assisted the human writers of the Bible in such a way that, while they remain real authors, God is the Bible's main author.

Irenaeus of Lyon, Saint, 207. Bishop of Lugdunum in Gaul, martyr, Church Father, and apologist in the second century. His episcopal lineage is traced to Saint John through Saint Polycarp of Smyrna, a disciple of John. Irenaeus acknowledged John as the Beloved Disciple and as the author of John's Gospel.

Jaspers, Karl, 292. German philosopher and psychiatrist (1883–1969). Jaspers rejected a personal God and viewed Jesus, Socrates, the Buddha, and Confucius alongside each other as "paradigmatic individuals" who have exerted the greatest influence on human history, as explained in his book *Socrates, Buddha, Confucius, Jesus: The Paradigmatic Individuals.*

Jeremias, Joachim, 21. German Lutheran Scripture scholar (1900–1979). He took a more positive view of the ability of scholarship to know the historical truth about Jesus in contrast to such scholars as Rudolf Bultmann, who were more skeptical. Jeremias' work on the parables of Jesus was especially influential. He also taught that Jesus thought the Kingdom of God was present in his ministry, but that the fullness of the Kingdom was yet to come.

"Jesus poem", 228. Term used by Pope Benedict, adopted from Martin Hengel, to contrast with "pneumatic Gospel". A "Jesus poem" is a fanciful creation of the author reflecting his own impression of Jesus and subject to the author's own foibles and faulty memory rather than being rooted in communion with Jesus through the Holy Spirit.

Johannine question, 222. Refers to the scholarly debate, going back at least to the third century, about the identity of the author of John's Gospel. Options include the Apostle John; a somewhat mysterious figure called John the Elder (or Presbyter John) mentioned in a fragment of a letter by the second-century bishop Papias; and an anonymous follower of the Apostle John. Some scholars refer to the eyewitness source for the Gospel of John as "the Beloved Disciple", whom many see as the Apostle John. The one who actually wrote down the material given by the Beloved Disciple is sometimes thought to be an associate of the apostle, perhaps Presbyter John. Benedict maintains that the Gospel of John goes back to eyewitness testimony, even if the Apostle John did not himself actually write the text we have now, but relied on another to write the content of John's testimony about Jesus.

John Chrysostom, Saint, 19. Fourth-century theologian and Doctor of the Church, Chrysostom was archbishop of Constantinople. He is known for his eloquence in preaching and for the liturgy that bears his name.

Judaizers, 118. Movement among Christians in the very early Church to require Gentile converts to adhere to the Mosaic Law. The Council of Jerusalem (see Acts 15) repudiated the position of the Judaizers. Saint Paul forcefully opposed them.

Jülicher, Adolf, 184. German biblical scholar (1857–1938) who emphasized the difference between allegory and parable. He held that parables are stories drawn from real life in order to communicate one and only one main point. Allegories, he said, were figurative stories and interpretations of stories devised to represent philosophical ideas. Based on the fact that some of Jesus' parables seem to have allegorical elements, Jülicher held that these were not parables of Jesus but later creations. Numerous scholars, including Benedict, have refuted Jülicher's conclusions.

Justin, Saint, 245. Early Christian saint, apologist, and martyr who converted to Christianity after trying out different philosophical sects; also called Justin Martyr.

Kolvenbach, Father Peter-Hans, 135. Jesuit spiritual writer and the twenty-ninth superior general of the Society of Jesus from 1983 to 2006. Kolvenbach was born in 1928 in the Netherlands.

Kuhn, Helmut, 198. Twentieth-century German scholar who taught at the University of Chicago.

Kyrios, 301. Greek word meaning "Lord". In the story of the abundant catch of fish (Lk 5:1–11), Peter calls Jesus "Kyrios" after the miraculous catch, before he had referred to him as *epistata,* a Greek word meaning "master" or "teacher". In the Greek translation of the Old Testament, *Kyrios* is the term used to refer to YHWH. When New Testament writers use it to refer to Jesus, they are generally underscoring his divinity.

Letter of Aristeas, 179. Second-century B.C. letter from Aristeas who was purportedly a courier of the king of Egypt, Ptolemy II Philadelphus. The letter related the story of the translation of the Hebrew Old Testament into Greek by seventy-two Jewish scholars at the command of Ptolemy. The story relates how each translator, working independently, arrived at the same translation, word-for-word, as the rest of his colleagues.

Levite, 196. Members of the Hebrew tribe of Levi charged with caring for the Tabernacle, serving in and guarding the Temple in Jerusalem, and assisting the Temple priests.

Lewis, C. S., 271. Prolific English man of letters, novelist, apologist, and member of the Church of England (1898–1963). Lewis abandoned Christianity as a young man but recovered his faith and became a vigorous defender of Christianity. Perhaps his most famous work of popular theology is his book *Mere Christianity.*

Logos theology, 253. The cornerstone of Philo of Alexandria's attempt to show the harmony between Platonic philosophy and Jewish faith, identifying the Greek idea of *Logos* as the first principle of the universe with YHWH.

Loisy, Alfred, 48. French Catholic modernist theologian (1857–1940). Loisy was dismissed from his teaching position and excommunicated for his adherence to modernist doctrines and his rejection of aspects of the Catholic faith. Loisy was famous for his comment that Jesus preached the Kingdom but what came was the Church.

Marxism, 31. Modern atheistic and materialistic system of thought developed by nineteenth-century Prussian philosopher and political activist Karl Marx (1818– 1883); promises the possibility of perfect earthly happiness as a result of the dialectic of history with no reference to afterlife or miraculous intervention.

Melchisedek, 253. The king of Salem identified in Genesis 14:18 as "priest of God Most High" to whom Abram offers a tithe. The Letter to the Hebrews speaks of

Christ as belonging to the priesthood after "the order of Melchizedek" (Heb 7:17), citing Psalm 110:4.

Messori, Vittorio, *Patì sotto Ponzio Pilato?*, 41. Book by the contemporary Italian journalist exploring the Passion and death of Christ.

metanorms, 125. Frank Crüsemann's term to describe apodictic law, meaning that apodictic law provides the norms for critiquing and revising casuistic law.

Moltmann, Jürgen, 53. German Protestant theologian born in 1926 who developed a "theology of hope" explicitly to address a Germany shattered by what it had done during the Holocaust, at the same time calling into question Christian doctrines such as the impassibility of God and conciliar formulations of the doctrine of the Trinity.

ne plus ultra, 73. Latin phrase meaning "apex" or "pinnacle"; literally, "nothing more beyond".

Neusner, Jacob, 69. Prolific Jewish theologian and rabbi born in 1932; author or editor of more than nine hundred books. His book *A Rabbi Talks with Jesus* greatly influenced the writing of *Jesus of Nazareth*.

Newman, Cardinal John Henry, 160. English theologian and Anglican priest (1801–1890) who converted to Catholicism from Anglicanism. Newman was a leader in the Oxford Movement, a movement within the Anglican church to bring it closer to its Catholic roots. He was later ordained a Catholic priest and eventually was made a cardinal in 1879. He was proclaimed "venerable" in 1991, and the cause for his canonization as a saint continues.

Nietzsche, Friedrich, 97. German classical philologist and atheist philosopher (1844–1900); Nietzsche repudiated Plato, Christ, and their followers as resentful enemies of human nobility. He viewed the Sermon on the Mount, for example, as expressing the envy of the weak and unsuccessful of this world who revel in curses upon the strong and the successful.

Origen, 41. Enormously influential theologian and biblical commentator of the second and early third centuries (c.185–253/254); Origen was educated and taught in Alexandria. Origen's most notable task was to put Greek thought at the service of Christianity.

Papias of Hierapolis, Saint, 225. Early second-century bishop of Hierapolis (in modern Turkey) and martyr who seems to distinguish between the Apostle John and a figure called John the Elder (or Presbyter John). This may indicate a "school" of disciples in Ephesus who followed the teaching of the Apostle John, whose teaching went into the Gospel that bears his name. Papias' book was a work, probably written around 130, on the sayings of Jesus. The text is now lost except for portions of it quoted by other ancient writers.

Papini, Giovanni, xi. Controversial Italian man of letters (1881–1956) whose *Life of Christ* influenced Joseph Ratzinger/Benedict XVI.

Passover, 21. Jewish feast commemorating the Exodus from Egypt (see Ex 12:1–20; Lev 23:5; Deut 16:1–8, 12). Jesus' Bread of life discourse (Jn 6:1–51) and the Last Supper (Jn 12:1; 13:1–2, 21–28) occur during the Passover.

Patrologia Graeca, 50. A 166-volume collection of the writings of the Church Fathers and some other contemporaneous figures.

Pesch, Rudolf, 173. German biblical scholar whose scholarship points to the Jewish sources of John's Gospel.

Pharisees, 13. Jewish movement founded after the Babylonian Exile known for its strict adherence to the laws and regulations of the Torah. In Jesus' time and before, the Pharisees strongly resisted the Hellenistic and Roman influence into Jewish life. The Pharisees often opposed the Sadducees, another group within Judaism. After the destruction of the Second Temple in A.D. 70, the Pharisaic sect became the basis for Rabbinic Judaism.

Philo of Alexandria, 253. Jewish philosopher in Alexandria, Egypt who lived around the time of Christ. He tried to show the harmony of Judaism and Platonic philosophy.

pied-à-terre, 225. A temporary or secondary home. From the French, meaning "foot to the ground".

Plato, 89. Classical Greek founder of philosophy in the West (429–347 B.C.); student of Socrates and teacher of Aristotle; author of *The Republic,* among other works.

"pneumatic Gospel", 235. Theological term affirming the historicity of a Gospel based on the communion of the author with Jesus, the subject of the Gospel, through the Holy Spirit. This term points to the ability of the Gospel to lead the reader past the externals into the deep interiority of the words and events that it narrates.

Pontifical Biblical Commission (PBC), xv. Originally, a committee of cardinals established by Pope Leo XIII in 1902 to consider the proper understanding and interpretation of the Bible. In 1971, the PBC ceased to be an organ of the Catholic Church's teaching office and became a consultative body under the Congregation of the Doctrine of the Faith, made up primarily of respected Catholic biblical scholars and theologians. Its *ex officio* president is the Prefect of the Congregation for the Doctrine of the Faith.

Pontius Pilate, 11. Prefect of the Roman province of Judea between A.D. 26 and A.D. 36, Pilate was the Roman official in charge of the execution of Jesus. At the end of his reign, Pilate was removed by the Roman emperor for his brutality. Pilate is present in all four Gospel accounts (Mt 27:1–26; Mk 15:1–15; Lk 23:1–15; Jn 18:28—19:16).

Pool of Siloam, 242. Rock-cut pool of water near Jerusalem where Jesus sent the man who was born blind for his healing (John 9:1–7). John notes that Siloam means "sent".

Presbyter John, 225. Also known as John the Elder, a figure mentioned in Papias' book on the sayings of Jesus. Presbyter John seems to have been a disciple of John the Apostle. Presbyter John may have been the head of a Johannine "school" in Ephesus and the author of the Second and Third Letters of Saint John. He may also have been involved with the writing of the Gospel of John.

Qumran, 13. Site of the discovery of the Dead Sea Scrolls. It was the dwelling place of the Essenes, a Jewish sect opposed to worship in the Herodean Temple in Jerusalem. There are some indications that John the Baptist and perhaps Jesus and his family were close to this community.

rabbinic literature, 57. Jewish writings on law, ethics, and tradition outside of the Bible.

rahamim, 139. Hebrew word literally meaning "womb", but also taken to refer to divine compassion.

recapitulate, 20. This word is used here to refer to the way in which Christ in his own life takes up all of human history—that of an individual, of Israel, and of the wider world—in order to bring about its redemption and salvation.

Rech, Photina, 240. Cloistered Benedictine nun and spiritual writer (1914–1983); wrote on liturgical and sacramental topics.

regnocentrism, 53. Literally, "centered on the kingdom". Refers to the idea that God, Christ, and the Church are too divisive to be the foundation of theology, instead substituting the Kingdom, understood as a world of peace, justice, and environmental responsibility.

Riesenfeld, Harald, 314. German Calvinist theologian of the twentieth century.

Roman Canon, 285. The first Eucharistic Prayer of the ordinary form of the Roman Rite of the Mass.

Ruckstuhl, E., 226. Twentieth-century German Scripture scholar who claims that Presbyter John was a guardian of the traditions of the Apostle John.

Rule of Saint Benedict, 131. The book of precepts written by Saint Benedict to regulate monastic life for monks; later adapted for use by women religious. The rule is directed to a communal life of prayer and work, or *ora et labora,* under an abbot.

Sadducees, 13. Jewish sect founded in the second century B.C., known for its denial of the afterlife, including the resurrection from the dead. The Sadducees at the time of Jesus were committed to the integration of Hellenism and Judaism and attempted to make the best of Roman rule. They often opposed the Pharisees.

sanctuary of Pan, 289. Pagan holy place at which Pan, the god of sheep and flocks, was worshipped. This sanctuary was located at the mouth of the Jordan River and was later the site for the Roman city established by Herod: Caesarea-Philippi, or modern Banias.

Schlier, Heinrich, 174. German Lutheran New Testament scholar and convert to Catholicism (1900–1978). He was a student of Rudolf Bultmann, but he came to the conclusion that the Church envisioned in the New Testament is the Catholic Church.

Schmidt, K. L., 52. Early twentieth-century German Protestant theologian who emphasized the role of the Christian community in salvation.

Schnackenburg, Rudolf, xii. German Catholic biblical exegete (1914–2002) who attempted to correct some of what he saw as the imbalances of historical-critical scholarship in order to support the Catholic faithful. Benedict supports his basic goal even though he disagrees with particular elements of Schnackenburg's interpretation.

Schneider, Reinhold, 135. German poet and man of letters (1903–1958). His works were banned by the Nazis during World War II.

Scholastics, 200. Scholars of the medieval universities largely concerned with the engagement between Christian theology (especially that of the Fathers of the Church) and Greek thought, (especially that of Aristotle, the classical Greek philosopher and student of Plato, the reintroduction of whose works into the West in the Middle Ages sparked an enormous scholarly ferment because Aristotle's works provide such a thorough treatment of every aspect of learning that his thought in its completeness and rigor was seen to rival Christianity). "Scholastic" comes from the Latin *scholasticus,* "man of learning", or "man of the school".

Schönborn, Cardinal Christoph, 271. Catholic Dominican theologian and archbishop of Vienna, Austria (b. 1945); primary editor of the *Catechism of the Catholic Church.*

Scriptura sola (sola Scriptura), 223. Latin phrase meaning "by Scripture alone"; Protestant tenet claiming that Scripture itself is the sufficient and clear basis for all Christian doctrine. This tenet is often used explicitly to discredit Catholic reliance on Sacred Tradition as well as Sacred Scripture.

Shema Israel, 57. Old Testament prayer found in Deuteronomy 6:4–5; 11:13; and Numbers 15:37–41. Observant Jews say this prayer twice daily. The word *shema* is the first word of the prayer, often translated, "Hear, O Israel, the Lord our God, the Lord is one" or "Hear, O Israel, the Lord our God, the Lord alone".

Smith, C. W. F., 186. Episcopalian minister and New Testament scholar (1905–1993). Argued that the "Jesus as a moral teacher" figure of some modern exegetes would never have been crucified.

Socrates, 292. Classical Greek philosopher (469–399 B.C.) known for his investigation of the human things, such as politics and ethics, and his examination of authoritative opinion. Socrates was parodied by Aristophanes in *The Clouds* and was the teacher of Plato and Xenophon. Socrates was executed by Athens on charges of refusing to acknowledge the gods of Athens, importing strange gods of his own, and corrupting the youth of Athens.

Son of Man, 109. Title used by Jesus for himself and only rarely by others with respect to Jesus (e.g., Acts 7:56). It has strong roots in the Old Testament, especially in the Book of Daniel (7:13–14). The figure of the son of man in Daniel shares in the authority of God, the Ancient of Days. Jesus uses the expression in this way to indicate his divine authority, not merely his human nature.

Sons of Thunder, 178. Nickname given to the apostles James and John by Jesus (Mk 3:17).

Stein, Edith (Saint Teresa Benedicta of the Cross), 91. Philosopher, adult convert to Catholicism from Judaism, and Carmelite nun and martyr (1891–1942). She took the name Teresa Benedicta of the Cross when she entered Carmel. As a philosopher, she was a well-regarded student of Edmund Husserl. Killed at Auschwitz in 1942, she was canonized in 1998.

Stuhlmacher, Peter, 55. German Protestant theologian and New Testament scholar born in 1926.

Sukkoth, 306. Hebrew word meaning "tabernacles". See glossary entry for "Feast of Tabernacles".

supersubstantialis, 154. Vulgate translation of the Greek word *epiousios*, which is found in the fourth petition of the Lord's Prayer (Mt 6:11); Latin word meaning "supersubstantial", referring to the new and superior "substance" that the Lord provides in Holy Communion.

Synoptic Gospels, 26. The Gospels of Matthew, Mark, and Luke; so-called because of their similar structures and use of much of the same material to narrate Christ's works and teachings. "Synoptic" means "same view".

Tertullian, 240. Influential Latin Christian writer and apologist; he converted to Christianity around 197 and was ordained a priest a few years later. Tertullian separated from the Catholic Church a few years and became part of the Montanist movement. He probably died without being reconciled to the Church.

theocentrism, 53. Theological view that God is the center of Christianity, as opposed to Christ (Christocentrism), the Church (ecclesiocentrism) or the Kingdom of God (regnocentrism).

Theophilus of Antioch, 93. Bishop of Antioch and apologist in the second century; author of *Against Autolycus.*

Thérèse of Lisieux, Saint, 76. French Carmelite saint and Doctor of the Church (1873–1897). Known as "the Little Flower", Saint Thérèse is known for her "Little Way", which emphasizes holiness in common, everyday actions.

Third Order, 79. Associates of a religious order who are usually laymen and who participate in the life of the order.

Torah, 13. Refers generally to the Law of Moses and specifically to the Pentateuch, the first five books of the Hebrew Scriptures: Genesis, Exodus, Leviticus, Numbers, and Deuteronomy.

Trinitarian dialogue, 282. The term as used by Benedict refers to the "dialogue" among the Persons of the Holy Trinity, especially between the Father and the Son. Benedict uses the term in connection with his interpretation of John 10:14–15: "I am the good shepherd; I know my own and my own know me, as the Father knows me and I know the Father; and I lay down my life for the sheep." Benedict understands Jesus here to refer to his bringing his disciples into communion with the Holy Trinity.

Tun-Ergehens-Zusammenhang, 75. German phrase referring to the causal relationship of one's moral conduct with the blessings or curses one experiences in life.

vom Bösen, 165. German translation of "from evil", part of the last petition of the Lord's Prayer (Mt 6:13). The phrase can be translated either "from evil" or "from the Evil one", referring to Satan.

von Harnack, Adolf, 7. German Protestant theologian and Scripture scholar (1851–1930) who did much to establish the use of the historical-critical method. He is famous also for attempting to "de-hellenize" Christianity by removing the influence of Greek thought and culture in order to return to what he regarded as a purer form of Christianity. He also argued that Christ's message did not proclaim himself but focused on the Father.

Vulgate, Saint Jerome's, 154. Latin translation of the Bible from the early fifth century. The Vulgate and its revisions have been the standard Latin Bible in the Catholic Church since its promulgation. *Vulgata* is a Latin word meaning "common".

Wholly Other, 24. Term referring to the doctrine of God's transcendence.

Wilckens, Ulrich, 223. Contemporary German Lutheran bishop and New Testament scholar (b. 1928) who has argued that the Beloved Disciple in John's Gospel was not a historical figure but a symbol. Benedict rejects his view as incompatible with the Gospel of John's presentation of the Beloved Disciple as an eyewitness of the events it describes.

Willam, Franz Michel, xi. Austrian pastor and theologian (1894–1981) who was mostly interested in John Henry Newman scholarship. Willam authored a work concerning the life of Christ, *The Life of Jesus in the Land and among the People of Israel*, which focused on Jesus' historical context and which made an impression on Joseph Ratzinger/Benedict XVI.

YHWH, 56. Transliteration of the Hebrew word for God, or "Yahweh"; also known as the Tetragrammaton, meaning "word of four letters".

Yom ha-Kippurim, 306. Better known as *Yom Kippur,* or the Day of Atonement. Leviticus 23:27 mandates this day of fasting for repentance. Before the Temple was destroyed in A.D. 70, the high priest would enter the Holy of Holies and pronounce the name of God, YHWH, and performed a series of sacrifices for the atonement for sins.

Zealots, 12. A militantly anti-Roman Jewish sect that lived and agitated in Palestine from at least the mid-first century B.C. until it was annihilated during the Roman destruction of the Jewish Rebellion, c. A.D. 70. At least one of the Twelve, Simon, called the Zealot, seems at some point to have been a Zealot sympathizer (Lk 6:15).